building
the
body

Text copyright © Pamela Evans 2002
The author asserts the moral right
to be identified as the author of this work

Published by
The Bible Reading Fellowship
First Floor, Elsfield Hall
15–17 Elsfield Way, Oxford OX2 8FG
ISBN 1 84101 193 2

First published 2002
10 9 8 7 6 5 4 3 2 1 0
All rights reserved

A catalogue record for this book is available from the British Library

Printed and bound in Great Britain by
Omnia Books Limited, Glasgow

building the body

the body

pamela evans

transforming relationships in the local church

Acknowledgments

I am delighted to be able to acknowledge the help and encouragement received from brothers and sisters in Christ as I have researched and written this book. Numerous Christians from a variety of church backgrounds have commented, questioned, challenged my thinking and shared their experience. I've seen the body of Christ in creative action as others have complemented my gifts and expertise with their own. This is certainly true of Revd Paul Dunthorne who commented on an early draft. I have benefited tremendously from his New Testament scholarship.

I shall always be grateful to Revd John Greed who in 1994, as Rector of St Helen's parish, channelled my enthusiasm by inviting me to teach the church's 'Bodybuilding Course'. The following year he was succeeded as Rector by Revd Chris Key, who has taught, enthused, encouraged and led by example as we have sought to apply the New Testament teaching on being the body of Christ. Translating theory into action is never as simple as it looks. I thank God for all who have decided to abandon the search for a perfect church and, in spite of all the 'untidiness', have committed themselves to working on our particular 'building site'! Special thanks to those members who have allowed me to tell snippets of their stories, and to all who gave feed-back on the group studies prior to the final draft.

Shirley Green, Margaret Milborrow and Barbara Wood have acted as my support group during the writing of this book. Their prayers, their listening ears, their wise comments and their encouragement have been invaluable. Lin Button has continued to enrich my spiritual journey. She has enlarged my understanding of numerous issues and exercised my sense of humour, as have Chris Key, Mary Key, Pam Goodman and the members of my house group.

The writing has been my responsibility, but I hope that the many who have contributed along the way will enjoy seeing the book in print, knowing that they have played a significant part.

Pamela Evans

Contents

Introduction 7
1 Normal Body Life 14
2 Together in Fellowship 28
3 Loved and Loving 42
4 Serving 61
5 Encouraging and Comforting 75
6 Building Up 92
7 Moving On Together 107
8 We Who Are Many Are One Body 130
Appendix: Listening Skills 154
Group Studies 171

From Christ, the Head, 'the whole body, joined and held together by every supporting ligament, grows and builds itself up in love, as each part does its work'.

EPHESIANS 4:16

Introduction

'We need each other.' What an old-fashioned idea! How out of tune with the culture of the self-made man and the liberated woman. And how risky! Neediness is associated with loss of face, with insecurity, with powerlessness. Exposing a need could bring feelings of vulnerability. Self-sufficiency feels safer than interdependence. The eye would prefer to be able to say to the hand, 'I don't need you!' (1 Corinthians 12:21).

The individualism which has characterized modern Western society has no doubt made its contribution but, in addition, Christians have at times seen needing one another as a sign of failing their Lord. Writing in the foreword to Myra Chave-Jones' book *The Gift of Helping* (IVP, 1982), John Stott voiced the concern then felt by many that confessing a need for human help could be taken as 'derogatory to Christ'. After all, Paul wrote, 'My God will meet all your needs according to his glorious riches in Christ Jesus' (Philippians 4:19). Should we not be seeing God's grace as sufficient? John Stott wrote:

Over the years I've come to see that these attitudes have more in common with Stoicism than with Christianity. Autarkeia was one of the Stoics' favourite virtues, 'self-sufficiency' or 'independence'. We Christians, however, should be honest and humble enough… to admit that we need each other. Paul did. Strong Christian leader that he was, he depended much on the loving support of his friends. During his final imprisonment he wrote expectantly of the second coming of Jesus; but meanwhile he longed for the coming of Timothy.

As Paul travelled, his teaching and preaching made a tremendous impact. Empowered by the Holy Spirit, his ministry transformed and enriched the lives of countless fellow believers. In turn, he received much from them, and not just when he was imprisoned. He seems to have valued the ministry of encouragement very highly. The New

Testament tells of Paul and other believers making long journeys in order to keep in touch and encourage one another—and this in an age in which primitive transport made it extremely hard work and time-consuming.

The way Paul behaved towards those he met on his travels complemented his spoken and written-word ministry. He clearly saw God-honouring relationships as an integral part of living the gospel: his letters contain numerous chapters and part-chapters on how to relate to one another. For example, the Christians in Ephesus are urged to 'Be kind and compassionate [KJV: tenderhearted] to one another, forgiving each other, just as in Christ God forgave you' (Ephesians 4:32). To the Roman believers Paul wrote that 'those of us who are strong and able in the faith need to step in and lend a hand to those who falter, and not just do what is most convenient for us. Strength is for service, not status. Each one of us needs to look after the good of the people around us, asking ourselves, "How can I help?"' (Romans 15:1–2, *THE MESSAGE*).

Paul's doctrinal teaching has served as a tremendous resource for the Church down the centuries, but his teaching on relationships has, I believe, been under-emphasized. The time has come to redress the balance. In particular, it's time for God's people to embrace all that it means to be the body of Christ (Romans 12:4–5; 1 Corinthians 12:12). Paul paints a powerful word-picture of the body—numerous parts with differing characteristics and capabilities, intentionally joined together, working with the head, concerned for one another, sharing in one another's suffering and rejoicing (1 Corinthians 12:14–26), each playing a role in 'body-building'.

It's a sobering thought that we too contribute to the lives of our brothers and sisters in Christ and to our community, whether or not we're aware of doing so. If our contribution isn't positive, it's likely to be negative, even if only in the sense of subduing any expectations of giving to or receiving from one another. 'Blessed is he who expects nothing, for he shall not be disappointed', as the bogus beatitude tells us. Expecting nothing, or very little, by way of edification or encouragement from ordinary fellow Christians may be seen by some as normal; ministry is the responsibility of the minority, and the tradition of congregational passivity is well-established in many churches. But is such a dynamic compatible with Paul's picture of interdependent members all playing their part as the body of Christ is built up? I don't believe it is.

The New Testament epistles overflow with exhortations. 'Love one another,' urges the elderly apostle John repeatedly (1 John), echoing Jesus' recurring emphasis in his final words to his disciples (John 13—15). In the letter to the Hebrews, the writer exhorts his readers to encourage one another and to spur one another on (Hebrews 3:13; 10:24–25). Writing to the Thessalonians, Paul says, 'Encourage one another and build each other up, just as in fact you are doing' (1 Thessalonians 5:11). The Galatians are told to restore gently those who have fallen into sin, and to carry one another's burdens (Galatians 6:1–2). Paul writes to the Colossians about teaching and admonishing one another with all wisdom (Colossians 3:16). There is much more in similar vein—addressed to whole churches rather than to a few leaders.

It's my experience that where members of the body of Christ work together at living out the biblical pattern of mutuality and healthy interdependence, much good comes of it. The scriptural principles of 'body life' can be applied within any denomination and in churches large or small—wherever there are Christians who are open both to New Testament teaching and to all that *koinonia* (fellowship, communion, communication) is intended to involve.

Relationships in demand

Social commentators tell us that the tide has turned. After years of striving to cut loose, there's a growing hunger for connectedness. Freedom is wonderful but, after a while, being out there alone, doing your own thing, can be lonely. Our post-modern society places a high value on relationships. What's more, spirituality is now firmly on the agenda. Relationships within which it is possible to explore the spiritual side of life are increasingly prized rather than despised.

Over the past two decades there has been an explosion of interest in counselling. Mentoring is now recognized as of value in both educational and business spheres, and is creeping into the Church. Spiritual direction, once sought by the few, is being recommended and pursued by many more. These trends reflect—among other things—a hunger for the mutual help and encouragement that has been neglected. So, should we be clamouring for more training courses, so that a greater number of experts can be equipped to serve us? Or could we re-examine the 'old-fashioned' way of doing things?

The Australian film character 'Crocodile' Dundee found many aspects of life in the USA mystifying, but perhaps none more so than the idea of someone visiting a professional for help with opening up about their difficulties. Incredulous, he asked what the matter was— didn't they have any mates? It saddens me that some Christians feel they have no choice but to turn to paid listeners because they cannot find brothers or sisters in Christ able and willing to help. Much of what folk appear to be looking for in specialist relationships is outstandingly ordinary—if that's not a contradiction in terms. There will always be a need for those with special training to help people whose difficulties are complex or overwhelming, but that doesn't mean that everyone else is obliged to watch from the sidelines. We mustn't allow our expert-orientated culture to convince us that because we can't do everything we can't do anything at all.

Looking back, I'm aware of God having used many 'transforming relationships' to work out his purposes in my life. Some have been with individuals, others with groups; some with my peers, yet others with people different from me in every respect. I've also seen the same principles at work in the lives of those around me, in particular in the lives of our two sons—now grown up and living away from home. I thank God that for both our children he has provided fellow members of the body of Christ who have built them up, and have helped them to face the challenge not to be conformed to the pattern of this world (Romans 12:2).

It's vital to build life-changing relationships in our church communities. But let's not fall into the trap of imagining that we need to do so simply to make them happier or more comfortable—or even more exciting—places to be. That would be to buy into the current preoccupation with consumer satisfaction and self-fulfilment. No, we do so in order that the fully functioning body of Christ can work as God intends, glorifying him and reaching out in his name to a lost and fragmented world.

There are difficulties, of course: fallen human beings make mistakes; sin distorts our relationships; friction occurs. Sometimes, regretfully, brothers and sisters in Christ come to the decision that they disagree too profoundly or are hurting too much to continue walking together. But this is no argument for abandoning the picture the Bible paints of life within the body of Christ in which, we are told, 'each member belongs to all the others' (Romans 12:5). Let's be alert to potential difficulties and incorporate healthy safeguards. Let's remember our own frailty and sinfulness, and that of others—even the acknowledged experts—but let us not give up trying to help each other along the way.

Growing up in Christ

In the days when I was in clinical practice, one of my responsibilities was to monitor children's growth and development. If a baby was failing to put on weight, or a schoolchild appeared to lack the development appropriate for their age, it was my job to ensure that they were carefully assessed and received all the necessary treatment or help. To borrow the medical terminology I might have used then, some folk in our churches have a spiritual 'growth deficit' accompanied by worrying 'developmental retardation'.

This isn't a new problem. The writer to the Hebrews complained to his readers that 'though by this time you ought to be teachers, you need someone to teach you the elementary truths of God's word all over again. You need milk, not solid food!' (Hebrews 5:12). Paul detected a similar lack of progress among the Christians at Corinth

(1 Corinthians 3:1–2). Are there church leaders today who are bold enough to write or to speak in similar vein to their congregations? And are church members willing to respond positively to such exhortation?

We all do well to ask ourselves: Are we living as part-time Christians, and happy as such? Do we really *want* to move on to maturity in Christ? Moving on is meant to be for all of us, not just for those in their spiritual infancy who know they have a lot to learn. When writing to the Christians at Philippi, Paul—their founding apostle and spiritual father—emphasized that he had not 'arrived' spiritually, adding, 'I press on to take hold of that for which Christ Jesus took hold of me' (Philippians 3:12). In none of Paul's letters, in fact nowhere in the New Testament, is there any sense that it's OK to opt for a static, undemanding style of discipleship if you don't want the bother of the more challenging, mobile sort!

In *Driven Beyond the Call of God* (BRF, 1999) I described the consequences of allowing emotional pain or problems with self-worth to remain in the driving-seat of our lives. I wrote in some detail about how Christian growth may be stunted by unhealthy ways of doing church. *Building the Body* offers an invitation to all who are ready to explore ways of giving and receiving encouragement, growing in faith and maturity, and gathering strength to meet the demands brought by commitment to Christ. It's for all who are willing for God to go on healing their wounds, which might otherwise cause them to be driven beyond or contrary to his will. It's about responding to God's call by being a working member of the multi-functional, multi-talented body of Christ.

As it's more difficult to work together fruitfully if communication is lacking, practical exercises for developing listening and other relevant skills are included. References to specialized 'transforming relationships' such as spiritual direction, counselling and mentoring, and suggestions for further reading, will flag up the possibility of additional help. The main emphasis, however, is on working to develop to full potential the ordinary everyday relationships within the body of Christ. A 'Focus Point' at the end of each chapter offers questions for reflection and raises possible practical applications of what has been covered. The group studies at the end of the book will enable you to explore some of the ideas with others, and to build up the body of Christ as you do so.

Normal Body Life

From [Christ, the Head] the whole body, joined and held together
by every supporting ligament, grows and builds itself up in love,
as each part does its work.

EPHESIANS 4:16

For as in one body we have many members, and all the
members do not have the same function, so we, though many,
are one body in Christ, and individually members one of another.

ROMANS 12:4–5 (RSV)

Sirens wail, lights flash. A high-speed journey to hospital, and an emergency operation. Nervous waiting to see if the reconnection of a severed thumb has been successful...

Down the road at the soccer stadium, a sidelined figure on crutches watches his team take on the opposition. It's only a knee injury, but his whole body is suffering from the restless nights due to the pain, not to mention the tension of being a spectator rather than a player. On the pitch, the forward's legendary left foot drives the ball into the back of the net. The scorer somersaults in delight...

Few of us will experience the trauma of a severed body part, but we all know that if one area of our body is suffering the rest usually suffers with it—and that our whole body can join in the celebrations of what one part has accomplished! We also take it for granted that different parts of our body have different functions. Without a second thought, we accept the diversity-in-combination which makes it what it is—a highly complex, multi-faceted creation... rather like the Church!

Part of Christ's body

When Paul wrote about 'the body of Christ' (1 Corinthians 12:27; see also Romans 12:4–5; Ephesians 1:22–23; 4:4–16, Colossians 1:18, 24; 2:19) he was using a tremendously powerful image which, centuries later, is still vivid. His message is a significant one for our generation which has tended to value independence and 'hanging loose' more highly than community and mutuality.

Securely connected to Christ the Head

Sadly, even some who would call themselves Christians feel that connectedness is grossly overrated. The freedom to remain dis-connected for long periods is their right, they say. They expect to slot back into 'their place' in the Church, but only when *they* are ready. But the importance of connectedness is a recurring theme in the New Testament, and not just in relation to other members of the body of Christ. In Matthew's Gospel we read how Jesus used a different word-picture to offer a connected working relationship with himself: 'Take my yoke upon you and learn from me' (Matthew 11:29).

Some folk find the whole idea of connectedness threatening because they've been in an abusive relationship; once hav-ing broken free, they see staying independent as their only hope of survival. The relationship Jesus offers can bring peace and hope into such fears and anxieties. It may, in time, endue wounded men and women with the courage necessary to play their full part in the body of Christ. If *you're* wary and bruised as a result of damaging past or present relationships, I'd encourage you to pray that Jesus will help you to know that he is not like those who have hurt you, and that he really can be trusted. 'I won't lay anything heavy or ill-fitting on you,' Jesus says. 'Keep company with me and you'll learn to live freely and lightly' (Matthew 11:29–30, *THE MESSAGE*).

Whatever our past experiences, a strong relationship with the good shepherd, the great high priest, the Head of the body, is vital if we're to remain connected when the other 'sheep' are irritable, the 'royal priesthood' is squawking like a bunch of seagulls, and the body seems intent on shooting itself in the foot! Eugene Peterson, with his gift for contemporary English idiom, has expressed some of the apostle Paul's inspired words as follows: 'We take our lead from Christ, who is the source of everything we do. He keeps us in step with each other. His very breath and blood flow through us, nourishing us so that we will grow up healthy in God, robust in love' (Ephesians 4:16, THE MESSAGE). If we lose touch with Christ the Head (fountainhead, sustainer), not only are our relationships dislocated, we're also deprived of the nourishment required to remain fully alive and growing. It's not just serious, it's life-threatening!

In the same way, when writing to the Colossians, Paul emphasizes the place of Christ as Head, the one in whom 'all things hold together'; 'from whom the whole body... grows' (see Colossians 1:17–18; 2:19). Whatever the structure of our own particular church, Christ is still the Head. Any tendency to allocate that role to a member or members of the body of Christ is to be fiercely resisted.

Diversity is essential

Some fear that being joined together means abandoning individuality, but distinctiveness is part of the plan! 'If the whole body were an eye, where would the sense of hearing be? If the whole body were an ear, where would the sense of smell be? But in fact God has arranged the parts in the body, every one of them, just as he wanted them to be. If they were all one part, where would the body be? As it is, there are many parts, but one body' (1 Corinthians 12:17–20). Paul leaves us in no doubt that he sees the diversity of the parts as a strength rather than a weakness.

Paul tells the Romans, 'Just as each of us has one body with many members, and these members do not all have the same function, so in Christ we who are many form one body, and each member belongs to all the others.' Note that he then continues, without a break, 'We have different gifts, according to the grace given us' (Romans 12:4–6). It's no coincidence that both these passages of teaching about the interdependent parts of the body of Christ—its diverse components united in one glorious whole—are placed alongside teaching on the diversity of spiritual gifts. (See also Ephesians 4:11–13.)

Just as 'each member belongs to all the others' (Romans 12:5), the spiritual gifts are given for the blessing of the whole body of Christ. This message comes across even more clearly in 1 Corinthians: 'There are different kinds of gifts, but the same Spirit. There are different kinds of service, but the same Lord. There are different kinds of working, but the same God works all of them in all men. Now to each one the manifestation of the Spirit is given for the common good' (1 Corinthians 12:4–7). There follows a list of gifts, ending with the words, 'All these are the work of one and the same Spirit, and he gives them to each one, just as he determines' (12:11). Paul continues, 'The body is a unit, though it is made up of many parts; and though all its parts are many, they form one body. So it is with Christ' (12:12).

Paul juxtaposes the teaching on diverse spiritual gifts and the individuality of the parts of the body in order that the ideas might complement and give weight to one another. Diversity is an intended feature of normal body life. (This theme is explored further in Study Session 1, page 172.) Some find it threatening, and on occasions the Enemy uses this as a lever to promote division. But the diversity is God-given, and given for our good. It reflects the nature of the Trinity, the supreme example of interdependent diversity in unity. We opt for uniformity at our peril.

Looking for growth

It's normal and healthy for human bodies to grow and develop until they reach maturity. Likewise, the body of Christ is expected to grow until Christ comes again. But note that it grows both 'as God causes it to grow' (Colossians 2:19) and 'as each part does its work' (Ephesians 4:16). Human bodies grow and develop properly only if their parts are being used. In the same way, the parts of the body of

Christ must be active if healthy growth is to take place.

Christian growth and development certainly need monitoring, but we don't have to become preoccupied with signs of progress or anxieties about its lack—in ourselves or others. An occasional pause for reflection, for example in the season of Lent or at the end of a year of housegroup or other meetings, is a good discipline. Others often see new growth of which we're oblivious, so setting aside some group time to review our individual and corporate journeying, and to ask God how he sees things, may be valuable.

When assessing growth, we must keep the emphasis on things that matter—matter to God, that is. Just as when assessing a child's growth we measure their height rather than the length of their hair or toenails, spiritual growth has to be measured against the one standard that really matters—that of Christ-likeness. The destiny to which God has called us is to be 'conformed to the likeness of his Son' (Romans 8:29). Whether we're doing better or worse than others doesn't come into it. We can't choose a course with less exacting aims; we have to accept God's syllabus, thankful that he is at work in us—doing all he can to make sure that we see it through (Philippians 2:12b–13).

Contributing to growth

Perhaps the first thing for any would-be grower or growth-helper to learn is that there's no instant recipe for growth! In real life, most significant changes involve a *process*; time is a necessary ingredient. Some periods in which nothing much seems to be happening are God-directed times—times of learning how to apply new knowledge, times of consolidation and strengthening. The Holy Spirit can bring miracles of growth at a breathtaking pace, and sometimes does just that, but most growth involves more than faith and an openness to God's Spirit: patience and perseverance have a part to play, too.

Genuinely barren times do occur. Some are due to a divided heart or straightforward disobedience, and repentance is necessary in order to move on. But lack of progress may also result from interference by the Enemy, who opposes growth and other signs of life as a matter of principle. If we are to give a helping hand to a brother or sister in Christ at such a time, we must pray for discernment and not make assumptions about the cause.

Contrary to what many seem to believe, we don't have to be experts in order to contribute to the building up of the body and the growth of the other parts. We don't have to be superhuman, a church leader, or even greatly experienced in the Christian life to offer help and encouragement. When we meet new Christians, the freshness of their faith or their eagerness to testify to miracles of answered prayer may blow away any 'cobwebs' we've accumulated, raising our expectancy. Young Christians who've just grasped an aspect of Christian truth can fruitfully remind others of it, their enthusiasm or clarity cutting through the fog of familiarity.

For example, some years ago the teenagers at our church had been studying the first few chapters of Paul's letter to the Romans. Our son Matthew was deputed to share their findings with the rest of the church in a Sunday evening service. This he did, closing with a pithy summary of the chapters, which made quite an impact: 'Sin: it's bad for you; don't do it.' I've thought about it many times since, and on occasions shared it with those for whom the seductiveness of sin appeared to be in danger of blurring the issue.

Sharing alongside

Also contrary to popular belief, our contribution doesn't have to be 'teacher style' or even in the form of words. It's easy to overlook other methods of communicating truths, values, support and so on. In past centuries, apprenticeship was the most significant transforming relationship in the lives of many adolescents. If we are truly in relationship with other members of the body of Christ, working and serving alongside one another, we may or may not have opportunities to share verbally what the Lord has been teaching us, but we'll certainly be able to demonstrate it in practical ways and by our attitudes and lifestyle.

Jesus' disciples lived and walked alongside him, seeing him in action privately as well as publicly. They saw him relating to men, women and children, to Jews and Gentiles; they observed his dealings with clever legal types who wanted to trip him up, and with outcasts whom everyone else sought to give a wide berth. They saw Jesus handle rejection, adulation, conflicting demands, weariness and much more. All this will have made a significant contribution to the equipping that later enabled them to teach and lead others. Many worthwhile things are more easily 'caught' than taught.

Jean Vanier, the founder of the first L'Arche community for mentally disabled people and their helpers, has written about some 'being alongside' relationships found within L'Arche.

In L'Arche we use the word 'accompaniment' in a way that is very unusual in English… we have not found a better way to express the reality of being alongside people as a companion and friend in order to help them grow in freedom and in the spirit of the community. 'Accompaniment' has its roots in the Latin cum pane, *eating bread together, which signifies a bond of friendship, a covenant.*

Vanier adds that 'many people need desperately to be able to communicate some of their inner pains and joys to someone who can hold them without making judgments, but with understanding, compassion and a certain wisdom… The essential aspects of… accompaniment are: listening, caring, clarifying, affirming and challenging… All this rests on a basis of trust' (Jean Vanier, *Community and Growth*, second revised edition, DLT, 1989).

Walking alongside others, urging them on, can only be done by the person we truly are. It's no use trying to send the person we'd like to be on that sort of journey; perfect but imaginary saints are no company at all—only the real, fallible human variety will do. Our culture prizes an impressive image more highly than a less glittering but truly worthwhile reality. God's kingdom turns this sort of thinking upside down: 'image' which is part of a façade rather than birthed in truth is part of the dross that must be purged away; it not only counts for nothing at all, it's actually offensive to God. For a more detailed look at the subject of 'keeping up appearances' see the chapter of that name in my book *Driven Beyond the Call of God* (BRF, 1999).

Sharpening or blunting?

If we're securely connected to the body of Christ, and daily experiencing God's grace, we've probably influenced others for good already. But if our own walk with God is distant, that too will have had an effect. Lives that mingle an appearance of piety with sharp practice in business, or conversation that intersperses God-talk with gossip, may be teaching things we'd prefer others not to be learning.

God in his mercy uses imperfect instruments to fulfil his purposes. None the less, if we're setting out to have a positive effect on the lives of those around us, it's imperative that we open our own lives to God's scrutiny—and listen to and act upon what he says. 'You use steel to sharpen steel, and one friend sharpens another,' says Proverbs 27:17 (*THE MESSAGE*). As I quickly learned when my grandfather showed me how to hone a blade on a steel, the effect of rubbing the two together can be blunting. If we're to make a worthwhile difference to those with whom we interact, we must welcome the Holy Spirit's influence on our own lives. Then we're more likely to be effective sharpeners, not blunters.

Mutual sharpening happens quite naturally as part of friendship, so I'm concerned that many Christians, especially those in leadership, feel they simply do not have the time to make—or to keep—real friends. Some even appear to have forgotten that friendship amounts to much more than encountering people at meetings! Friendship is one of God's good gifts to humankind, for our well-being and our integrity's sake, not just for our enjoyment. Good friends love us as we are, but also love us enough to let us know when the choices we're making seem to be taking us into dubious territory. If our lives are too busy to develop and maintain healthy same-sex friendships (and, if we're married, to keep friendship alive in that context, too), we're definitely too busy: urgent action is required before it's too late.

Owning our limitations

The body of Christ is made up of real men, women and children living real lives, many of them frustrated by their own limitations. All human beings have limitations—in knowledge, experience, reasoning ability, physical capacity, endurance and so on. I can only be in one place at a time and, although my children sometimes doubted this, I do not have eyes in the back of my head! None of us has the capacity to be fully engaged with every single member of the body of Christ simultaneously. The only one who is omnipresent, omniscient and omnipotent is God. He has promised to equip us with all that we need, and at times this enables us to go beyond what might have been thought possible. But we're still human, not superhuman. In short, God is God and we are not; woe betide us if we forget that distinction.

Of course, I could be reminding you that God's power is made perfect in our weakness. 'When I am weak, then I am strong,' said Paul (2 Corinthians 12:10). Absolutely! But if asked about your weaknesses, how would you respond? Paradoxically, we may be most vulnerable in the areas in which we feel most capable. When we're fully in control, we may neglect to listen for and submit to God's leading and to draw on the resources he provides. As Paul warns elsewhere, 'If you think you are standing firm, be careful that you don't fall!' (1 Corinthians 10:12).

We may use the word 'weaknesses' to describe the areas of failure we'd prefer God to take away but, alongside God's mighty power, even our greatest strengths look pretty puny. Yes, we can thank God for the gifts and abilities he has given us, and use them with the sort of confidence that gives him glory, but we need to remember that our strengths may become weaknesses or even downright liabilities if used without reference to the Giver.

Paul's understanding seems to have been that God allowed him his 'thorn in the flesh' (whatever that was) to prevent him from 'becoming conceited' (2 Corinthians 12:7). It appears that through it he became glad to own up about his weaknesses, which served as open doors to God's power in his life, and he learned to welcome all sorts of difficulties (12:9–10). Do we have the same approach? I confess that I'm more likely to pray for release from difficulties and weaknesses than to welcome them!

Connected and fruitful

Another picture of connectedness given by Jesus is that of the vine. 'I am the true vine... Remain in me, and I will remain in you. No branch can bear fruit by itself; it must remain in the vine. Neither can you bear fruit unless you remain in me' (John 15:1, 4). The growth and fruitfulness are related to the connectedness. You may have heard the opening verses of chapter 15 of John's Gospel preached as an exhortation to bear much fruit, but it isn't! It's Jesus' ever-so-simple explanation of the dynamics of fruitfulness: remain in me and you'll bear fruit; go it alone and you won't—'apart from me you can do nothing' (15:5).

In the Vine and bearing fruit

God does look for fruit, but only in the sense that he knows it will be appearing if the conditions for fruitfulness are being met. Fruitfulness brings glory to our Father, the gardener (John 15:1, 8), and flows from a securely connected relationship with Jesus. Unfruitful, disconnected branches are only fit for the bonfire (15:6). Wise spiritual directors and other growth-nurturers encourage those who come to them to strengthen their connectedness with Christ; they don't just stress the importance of seeing fruit. Prayer and other activities will be a part of this strengthening, both as channels for God's grace and as outworkings of the growing relationship with Christ, but as we seek to encourage one another in fruitfulness, let's remember that it's primarily the connectedness that brings the fruit, not the activities.

As any good gardener will tell you, one of the secrets of fruitfulness is appropriate pruning—appropriate in timing, degree, and knowledge of the type of plant. My father gets teased about his pruning technique. Plants look like disaster-struck shadows of their former glory when he's finished with them. But he takes it in good heart, because *he* knows that's why his plants do so much better than ours!

Jesus taught his disciples that 'every branch that does bear fruit [my Father] prunes so that it will be even more fruitful' (John 15:2b). I confess that when my heavenly Father prunes me I'm inclined to whinge. But at such times I try to seek out other members of the body of Christ who will urge me to hang on in there. Those who merely sympathize or—worse still—suggest creative ways of avoiding what God is doing in my life are to be given a wide berth.

Today's society conditions us to see ourselves as consumers. (Are we happy with our position? Are we comfortable with our fellow branches? Have we ticked the 'pruning' or 'non-pruning' box?) God calls us to union with Christ, which inevitably unites us with our fellow branches. We also need to be prepared for the pruning required to transform us into fruitful branches—pruning away not just dead wood but healthy shoots and *much that to us seems good and worth preserving*. The connectedness and the pruning are integral parts of the package; Jesus' words don't appear to offer a less demanding option.

When preaching on the subject of pruning, Roger, our church warden, spoke about how he had enjoyed participating in sport at school and college. When he became a teacher he was required to undertake coaching on a Saturday, leaving Sunday as the only day on which he could play himself. Sunday sport would have prevented his involvement in Christian youth work. Looking back after many years of fruitful commitment in that sphere, he can see that although he was good at sport and it was a healthy activity, the loss of it was part of God's pruning. The sport was good, but it would have prevented the youth work which—for him, at that time—was God's 'best'.

The fruit of obedience

'If you obey my commands, you will remain in my love,' says Jesus (John 15:10). This is not to be interpreted as a manipulative state-ment, along the lines of 'Do as I say and then I'll love you'. It's encouragement to 'stay always within the boundaries where God's love can reach and bless you', as Jude puts it (Jude 21, Living New Testament).

Obedience is necessary for fruitfulness, and we'll be thinking more about encouraging one another in obedience in chapter 4. For the moment, let's just consider whether we have a preference for marshalling our own ideas, planning great things in God's name, and then offering him the fruit of our efforts—expecting him to round it all off nicely with his blessing. Do we sometimes need to encourage one another to slow down, so that God is able to tell us what *he* has in mind, before we embark on great projects in his name?

'No branch can bear fruit by itself; it must remain in the vine,' warns Jesus (John 15:4). Each branch of the vine needs the life-giving sap rising up through it in order to bear fruit, and when it does so it bears *only grapes*—fruit that reflects the character of the vine. Here this particular illustration reaches its limit, because it cannot convey the multitude of varieties of fruitfulness within the body of Christ, but it can be used to emphasize the defining characteristic of all fruit—that it reflects its origins.

'Fruit' originating in a need to be doing something (maybe even a need to execute a grand plan on a superhuman scale?) will reflect its origins in neediness. That's not to deny that God uses human creativity in the fruit-bearing process—he does. He made us creative beings, and he delights to use our creativity for his purposes. But our creative activity has to be directed and nourished by him: the branch is only fruitful as it is held in position and supplied with sap by the vine.

Put like that, bearing fruit sounds so easy—just sit there, and the sap will flow and the fruit will come! Why doesn't it feel that easy? In my experience, the struggle is usually related to the obedience. When we daily choose obedience—and choose obedience to what God has said, rather than to what we think God ought to have said—we experience a counter-pressure from the world, the flesh and the devil. This counter-pressure is a major element in the struggle. Another element is the choosing to go on being obedient when the fruit takes longer than we had bargained for. In both cases, our relationships within the body of Christ can help us to persevere, if we allow them to do so. As we move on to look at how this might work in practice, let's ask God to make us more aware of those around us who might be willing to lend—and receive—a hand.

Focus Point

After each chapter, this section is given as an aid to reflection. Use as many or as few of the questions as you find helpful.

- How do I feel about belonging, connectedness, interdependence, mutual help?
- Am I aware of being connected to Christ the Head, but not to 'the body'? Or connected to the church, but not to Christ?
- Are there types of people with whom I would prefer not to be connected in the body of Christ? Younger people? Older people? Men? Women? Those who belong to groups with whom you've had difficult encounters in the past, for example, bank managers, police officers, former school bullies, teachers? Bring your thoughts and feelings to God, and ask him to speak to you about them.
- Remembering the paradox that we may be most vulnerable in the areas in which we feel most capable... Am I ever tempted to see myself as an expert in certain areas, who only occasionally needs a little assistance from God?
- Do I really want to be fruitful? Or would I rather be comfortable... happy... popular?

Further reading

After each chapter, this section lists Bible passages and/or books which could be used to explore further the issues raised, if required.

Romans 12; 1 Corinthians 12; Ephesians 4:1–16.

Together in Fellowship

If we walk in the light... we have fellowship with one another.
1 JOHN 1:7

Make every effort to keep the unity of the Spirit through the bond
of peace. There is one body and one Spirit.
EPHESIANS 4:3–4

Some years ago, I visited a seaside church while on holiday. The small congregation was distributed throughout the cavernous building. I smiled at a lady nearby. She looked alarmed. Everyone else seemed to be doing their best to avoid eye contact. We were all in the same place at the same time, and outwardly doing similar things, but there was no sense in which we were worshipping *together*.

Together—or in parallel?

Are we prepared to go against what some would hold is a respected tradition of privacy in matters of religion? Dare we journey genuinely together with, not just in parallel with, others? Going in the same direction is not the same as travelling together; the defining characteristic of parallel lines is that they never meet, even if they run alongside one another for miles.

We may find it more agreeable to journey independently, but the biblical picture of the distinct yet interconnected parts of the body of Christ rules out this option. Furthermore, if we're to follow the biblical pattern, we must accept not only the idea of travelling together but also the need to work at being a positive influence in the lives of those around us.

Together in vulnerability, joy and suffering

If we're serious about walking alongside fellow travellers and building relationships that God can use to transform us and others, we're going to have to make a commitment to openness. Sooner or later, that will bring the pain of vulnerability. Openness plus vulnerability doesn't mean telling everything to everyone all the time! But it does mean telling a few folk about what's really important to *us*—not just hiding behind a worthy interest in what's important to others. For example, if we're brimming over with emotion at the arrival of a new grandchild, it would be odd not to mention it; we'd be depriving others of an opportunity to share our joy.

Opening up feels risky. Supposing I share my joys, my hopes and dreams, and everyone yawns and changes the subject? But it's vital that we do take the risk, for everyone's sake, not just ours. No less important is the sharing of grief, disappointments and failures. It's scriptural to 'mourn with those who mourn', too (Romans 12:15). We'll be looking further at the subject of walking alongside others who are hurting in Chapter 5, but for now let's consider how the depth of our fellowship may be affected by the way we handle our own suffering.

In order to grow in fellowship, we must be prepared to be open about our gloomy patches with those around us—and when the struggles are in progress, not just when they're gloriously resolved. From time to time I hear a testimony from someone I know, thanking God for his mercy in bringing to an end a prolonged period of adversity about which I knew nothing. If it becomes apparent that no one else knew anything about it either, I feel deeply saddened. Did the suffering have to be endured alone? The body of Christ would appear to have been deprived of an opportunity to 'be the body'—to support an injured part, to offer practical assistance, to pray for healing, or to influence the difficult patch in some other way. 'If one part [of the body of Christ] suffers, every part suffers with it' (1 Corinthians 12:26). If we're genuinely connected to other parts of the body of Christ, that will be our corporate experience.

Receiving as well as giving

Jesus is reported by Paul to have said that 'it is more blessed to give than to receive' (Acts 20:35). Some hear this as 'It's a sin to receive'. This may be because the teaching they've heard has majored on giving, as a corrective to selfishness. Well-rounded teaching on helping within the body of Christ will also emphasize the need to receive, not least because an unwillingness to do so may be rooted in pride.

Have you ever considered the fact that Jesus the Son of God was often on the receiving end of others' giving? For example, he asked Simon Peter to let him use his fishing boat as a speaking platform when people were crowding around him (Luke 5:3); he accepted hospitality in numerous homes; he asked the woman at the well for a drink, having no means to draw water for himself (John 4:7, 11); he borrowed a colt to ride into Jerusalem, and let others spread their cloaks over it before he sat on it (Mark 11:3, 7); he allowed a woman to anoint him 'for burial' (Mark 14:8); he borrowed a room so that he and his disciples could eat the Passover meal (Mark 14:14); I could go on...

Receiving hospitality and practical assistance may be acceptable, but what about allowing others in the body of Christ to come alongside when we're distressed? Even the thought of allowing anyone close at a distressing time is more than some can bear; it feels unsafe, perhaps because of damaging past experiences. For others it may feel like letting the side down: might friends be shocked or disappointed if they found out how needy and vulnerable—and how human— I really am? Contrast this with Paul's attitude (for example, 2 Timothy 4:9–11), and with the way Jesus behaved.

Willing to allow others to minister to us

On the night before his crucifixion, Jesus took Peter, James and John with him, leaving the remaining disciples at a distance. His three close friends observed that he was in deep distress. 'My soul is overwhelmed with sorrow to the point of death,' he told them. 'Stay here and keep watch' (Mark 14:34). The same passage goes on to relate how, while Jesus was a short distance away agonizing in prayer, the disciples were falling asleep. They were unable to give him much by way of support—but he did ask.

Jesus could have justified spending that night alone, telling himself that they'd never understand and that asking them to pray wouldn't do any good. But he didn't. If we're ever tempted to argue that suffering alone is the 'grown up' way to do it, or that no one is likely to be able to help, can we remember Jesus' example? Asking a few others to stand with us when we're wrestling with something lays us open to the pain of disappointment if they're unable to help as we'd hoped. However, in the longer term it may bring benefits such as greater understanding or closeness. They may even learn something through their feelings of inadequacy when faced with our difficulties. I wonder what Peter, James and John learned from that dreadful night.

Jesus' response in the face of imminent crucifixion was the prayer to 'Abba, Father' that the scriptures record (Mark 14:36) and from which we may all learn. In a much smaller way, those around us at our difficult times may be able to learn from the way we handle disappointment, failure and pain. If our difficulties turn us—and others—to prayer, that will draw us and them closer to the Father. If our response to pain is to lash out at those around us, we'll cause a lot of distress. But that too can be a growing experience if everyone is committed to seeing it through, and sharing forgiveness when the time is right.

The housegroup to which I belong suffered a major upheaval when the leader and assistant leader both lost close relatives in the same week. They had to take time out to mourn with their families, and to see to the numerous practical arrangements that crowd in at the time of a death. Their circumstances were very different, their way of handling things was very different, but both of them at various stages managed to communicate to the rest of us just how difficult they were finding it. The effect on the group was dramatic. In the space of a couple of weeks, we were drawn closer to one another and to the Lord. Our group times of prayer came alive in a new way as we interceded for those we loved who were in pain, and for their families. And group members grew visibly in faith, in love, in willingness to take responsibility, in understanding of what it means to be part of the body of Christ. Looking back some weeks later, we were able to thank God for bringing so much good out of a painful time.

Walking together as God's children

There's a sense in which it's easier to 'be in fellowship' with those with whom we have little contact: they're less likely to upset us! A half-remembered verse from my childhood goes something like this:

> *To live in love with saints above,*
> *How great will be the glory;*
> *But to live below with saints we know—*
> *Now that's a different story!*

Christian fellowship has the capacity to go beyond ordinary friendship. Through the ability to see others as God sees them, through the miracle of God's *agape*-love at work in our hearts, it can include those whom others see as unlovely, and those with whom we would not naturally form a bond. Relationships within the body of Christ are able to transcend cultural and social boundaries because their foundation is relationship with Christ, not natural friendship preferences.

Towards the end of the period of upheaval in our housegroup, one of the members commented that we were unlikely to be found together were we not all Christians—and we agreed! Our ages, backgrounds and personalities differ widely, and we don't always see things the same way. But we're children of the same heavenly Father, we serve the same Lord and Master, and are filled by the same Holy Spirit. 'There is one body and one Spirit' (Ephesians 4:4). That brings a depth of unity which may be missing in groups relying on having similar interests or personalities to keep them united.

Children of light

John draws attention to another aspect of the foundation for our relationships when he writes, 'God is light; in him there is no darkness at all. If we claim to have fellowship with him yet walk in the darkness, we lie and do not live by the truth. But if we walk in the light, as he is in the light, we have fellowship with one another' (1 John 1:5–7). Walking in the light is the basis for Christian fellowship, for *walking together*.

The second half of Paul's letter to the Ephesians has much to say on this and other aspects of relating to others. 'Live a life worthy of the calling you have received,' urges Paul. 'Be completely humble and gentle; be patient, bearing with one another in love. Make every effort to keep the unity of the Spirit through the bond of peace' (Ephesians 4:1–3). Paul continues with some highly specific teaching about which behaviours and attitudes are and are not acceptable from those who are 'all members of one body' (4:25). He sums up by urging them to 'live as children of light' and 'have nothing to do with the fruitless deeds of darkness' (5:8, 11). After exhorting his readers to go on being filled with the Holy Spirit rather than alcohol, Paul puts forward a model of using scripture, hymns, songs and 'music in your heart' to give thanks and praise to God together (5:19–20).

Submitting to one another

After saying all this, and before moving on to teaching directed at particular groups within the body of Christ (wives and husbands, children and parents, slaves and masters), Paul slips in a verse which is sometimes ignored. It sets the context for what follows, and indeed lays the foundation for all relationships: 'Submit to one another out of reverence for Christ' (Ephesians 5:21).

Mutual submission sets the tone. Some teaching on the sub-mission of wives to husbands fails to mention this. With mutual submission as the backdrop for all other submissions, relationships within the body of Christ should stand in sharp contrast to the world's hierarchical model in which the 'top dog' protects his or her position—as does the mid-range dog-with-aspirations, not wanting to be overtaken by the up-and-coming mongrel.

Servanthood as demonstrated by Jesus (Mark 10:45; John 13:14–15; Philippians 2:7) is to be our model for living. If we're submitting ourselves to his lordship and to one another, other revolutionary characteristics of body-of-Christ relationships, such as mutual acceptance (Romans 15:7) and bearing with one another even in failings (Romans 15:1), are more likely to blossom.

Forgiving one another

'Bear with each other and forgive whatever grievances you may have against one another. Forgive as the Lord forgave you' (Colossians 3:13). Given that the body of Christ is made up entirely of sinners, there will be a continuing need for forgiveness. If we fail to forgive, division will soon occur—first between two brothers or sisters in Christ, and then between groups as others take sides. In forgiving, as in other aspects of life, we're taught to take our lead from Christ. The standard is an exacting one.

Paul's second letter to the Christians at Corinth includes a para-graph referring to a particular issue of forgiveness that was troubling the church there (2 Corinthians 2:5–11). The requirements of church discipline having been seen to, Paul exhorts his brothers and sisters in Christ to forgive, and to underline that they have done so by reaffirming their love for the person concerned. (The Greek word translated 'reaffirm' in verse 8 may include a specific event such as a public reconciliation.) He concludes by saying (vv. 10–11), 'And what I have forgiven—if there was anything to forgive—I have forgiven in the sight of Christ for your sake, in order that Satan might not outwit us. For we are not unaware of his schemes.' This is the nub of the matter: division in the body of Christ serves Satan's purposes, not God's.

It must be obvious that it would be an uphill struggle to teach a new Christian about the biblical basis for forgiving one another if, in their church, many members would die rather than forgive those who left to form a 'rival' fellowship ten years ago (for example). Unwillingness to forgive makes it well nigh impossible for Christians to move on together—even to be truly together, moving on or not. Forgiveness is part of the 'climate' or 'atmosphere' of the Kingdom of God. Every time we forgive, it's as if we breathe a refreshing breath of Kingdom air into our community; every time we refuse to forgive, we allow the fetid breath of the Evil One to contaminate the air the whole community has to breathe.

Forgiving and forgiven

Jesus taught his disciples that if they were in the middle of offering a gift to God and they remembered that their brother had something against them, they should leave the offering in order to make reconciliation their priority (Matthew 5:23–24). He emphasized the centrality of forgiveness to Kingdom life when he taught his disciples to pray using what has become known as the Lord's Prayer (Matthew 6:9–13; Luke 11:2–4).

In Matthew's version, the sentence asking for forgiveness 'as we have also forgiven' is elaborated on in the following verses (Matthew 6:14–15). Eugene Peterson expresses it like this in THE MESSAGE: 'In prayer there is a connection between what God does and what you do. You can't get forgiveness from God, for instance, without also forgiving others. If you refuse to do your part, you cut yourself off from God's part'. (See also Mark 11:25.)

The same point was made by Jesus when, after telling Peter that he must forgive 'seventy times seven' (far too many times to count), he told the parable of the unmerciful servant. After receiving mercy when he was unable to pay a large debt, the servant refused even to allow extra time for repayments in the case of someone who owed him a trivial sum (Matthew 18:21–35). Accepting God's forgiveness while refusing to extend forgiveness to others just isn't on.

It's worth pondering why so many people find it hard to believe that God really is willing to forgive them. Could it be, at least in part, that they know what's in their hearts when they think about forgiving those who have wronged them? Might they be projecting their own reluctance to forgive on to God?

Other parts of scripture make it clear that our righteous God is able to extend forgiveness to us only because Christ, on the cross, paid the penalty that was our due. No one can earn God's forgiveness merely by forgiving others; those who seek God's forgiveness have to accept Christ's sacrifice on their behalf and put their trust in him. However, a wilful refusal to forgive others indicates that we have no real desire to live and breathe in the Kingdom climate. It's a rejection of God's plan. Earlier in the Sermon on the Mount, Matthew recorded Jesus' teaching that the way of the Kingdom is to love enemies and pray for persecutors. If we follow this teaching, the 'family likeness' will be recognizable in us—we'll be living as our Father's children should be living (Matthew 5:44–45). Luke recorded how Jesus showed this attitude even when he was being crucified (Luke 23:34).

When forgiveness feels impossible

If we or those we love have suffered serious harm at the hand of another, forgiveness may be very difficult. This is particularly so if we're living daily with long-term consequences, or the person concerned is continuing to make life unpleasant for us. We can pray, 'Lord, please help me to forgive', or even, 'Lord, please help me to be willing to be helped to forgive'. By praying in such a way, we show that we are choosing to align ourselves with God's will. In due course, by God's grace, we'll be enabled to face the choice to forgive —a choice of our will, not a matter of feelings. Remember, forgiving someone doesn't mean saying that what they did to us didn't matter or didn't hurt us. We can acknowledge the harm done to us, yet still choose to forgive.

After the 1939–1945 war, Corrie ten Boom cared for those who had suffered at the hands of the Nazis. She found that survivors who chose to forgive those who had harmed them were able to move on and rebuild their lives, regardless of the remaining physical scars; those who did not remained bitter and continued as invalids. The choice to forgive, painful though it may be, can bring a freedom that speeds the journey to wholeness. Medical research has demonstrated the beneficial effect of forgiveness, even when the forgiving is done without reference to God.

Whenever I'm finding my relationship with someone difficult for any reason (not just a matter of forgiveness), I find that praying for them daily makes a great difference. By 'praying for them', I mean praying for their well-being—not simply that they will stop being so hurtful or irritating! I pray for them that the Lord will bless and prosper them and give me opportunities to show them his love in action. If they are Christians, I pray that the Lord will help me to honour them as his much-loved children. It's not always easy to pray in this way, but my experience is that the Lord honours obedience.

Together in pilgrimage

'Blessed are those whose strength is in you, who have set their hearts on pilgrimage' (Psalm 84:5). This psalm gives a helpful picture, reminding us as it does that we're meant to be purposefully moving on in God's strength. Centuries ago when pilgrimage was a more accepted part of life, travelling alone (for any purpose, not just as a pilgrim) was relatively unusual; people tried to avoid it because they knew they'd be vulnerable to highway robbery. In our generation, independent travel is regarded as nothing out of the ordinary. In fact, many who travel in trains and buses prefer to act as if travelling alone, even if they are sardined with dozens of others!

Accepting the challenge

As I mentioned at the start of the chapter, I discovered that it's possible to have a similarly independent approach to worship. If the body of Christ is to be truly 'together', such attitudes will need to be challenged, as will some of today's other cultural norms. You could ask the Lord to draw attention to any patterns of thought or behaviour that you've absorbed from the culture around you, which may be hindering your worship, your discipleship or your relating to others within the body of Christ. Study Session 2 (pages 174–176) explores further what it means to be 'together as one'.

John Bunyan's 17th-century hymn 'Who would true valour see' echoes through my mind as I write. Each verse ends with the words '...to be a pilgrim'. I remember it from school assemblies, where we solemnly sang that we would 'labour night and day' to be one. Other hymns from my schooldays, such as 'Through the night of doubt and sorrow onward goes the pilgrim band', left me in no doubt that pilgrimage was hard work!

For a start, pilgrimage (literal or metaphorical) required, and still requires, a willingness to embrace change—something many of us find difficult. The circumstances and challenges of tomorrow are likely to be different from those we've faced today. For many folk, the most significant challenge is to cooperate with the Holy Spirit as he works to bring change on the inside. Whether or not we see ourselves as pilgrims, we do need to heed the call to faithful daily moving on as children of God, becoming the women and men God created us to be.

Together in 'hospitality, teaching and midwifery'

Margaret Guenther, an ordained priest and the Director of the Center for Christian Spirituality in New York, has written helpfully about spiritual direction. She makes it clear that the benefits of this special relationship extend well beyond those of friendship, not least because of the degree of detachment it affords. Nevertheless, her word-pictures of what happens within spiritual direction may be illuminating as we consider how sisters and brothers in Christ may help one another. Guenther writes about spiritual direction as 'hospitality, teaching and midwifery' (Margaret Guenther, *Holy Listening—The Art of Spiritual Direction*, DLT, 1992).

The hospitality Guenther has in mind (and which Peter commends—1 Peter 4:9) has little in common with the lavish entertaining which sometimes goes by that name today. It has more to do with the heart-welcoming of guests and the attention to their needs which pilgrims of old might have found in the monastic hospices *en route*. Writing about the Rule of St Benedict, used by Benedictine communities, Esther de Waal comments: '"Let everyone that comes be received as Christ", that most familiar phrase of the Rule, at once says that hospitality means more than simply the open door, and the place at table; it means warmth, acceptance, enjoyment in welcoming whoever has arrived.'

Esther de Waal goes on to note that after the hospitality has been given, 'St Benedict faces us with two very simple questions: Did we see Christ in them? Did they see Christ in us?' (Esther de Waal, *Seeking God*, Fount, 1984). Try carrying these questions with you for a few days, to see how they influence the way you relate to those with whom you come into contact.

As we'll continue to see throughout this book, there's more to teaching than standing at the front and holding forth! And midwifery...? While training to be a doctor I was required to deliver twenty babies. It was a privilege to be alongside during the pain and struggles of labour and to be the one who, medically speaking, brought each new life to birth. What a wonderful picture of how we can minister to one another during the pain and struggles of sanctification ('holy-making'). (See Paul's attitude, Galatians 4:19.)

Let's pray that we will be able to reveal Christ to one another, helping each other to hear and respond to God. As we walk alongside, we can teach by example things we've learned—or are in the process of learning. And, if we're open to being led by the Holy Spirit, we may play a part as new works of God's grace are brought to birth in others' lives. We can pray that these things will happen within our relationships... if we're willing to risk it, that is!

Focus Point

- When I think about embarking on or continuing a spiritual journey involving change, pressing on, moving on, I feel... what? Excited... apprehensive... weary...? Talk to God about your feelings. Ask him to help you as you consider what sort of next steps he might be asking you to take. You may find it worthwhile to reflect on the differences between pilgrimage and tourism.
- What effect am I having on the spiritual lives of those around me? Am I travelling genuinely together with fellow Christians, or would 'in parallel' better describe my relationships? Try carrying this question with you through the coming week. Remember that your impact will not be through words alone. If you become aware that all has not been as it should, confess this to God. Ask for his forgiveness and his help in living life his way.
- Are any of my relationships difficult because of problems with unforgiveness? If you're willing to try to forgive, ask your heavenly Father to help you to make a start. If your wounds are deep or the difficulties longstanding, you may need to ask a minister or counsellor for assistance. Try to find someone who has the necessary training and experience in addition to a willingness to help. The Association of Christian Counsellors (173a Wokingham Road, Reading, Berkshire RG6 1LT) may be able to give you a list of accredited counsellors in your area.

Further reading

Anne Long, *Approaches to Spiritual Direction*, Grove Spirituality Series No. 9, Grove Books, Third Edition, 1998.

Ecclesiastes 4:9–12; Mark 14.

Loved and Loving

May the Lord make your love increase and overflow for each
other and for everyone else, just as ours does for you.
1 THESSALONIANS 3:12

Go after a life of love as if your life depended on it—because it
does.
1 CORINTHIANS 14:1 (*THE MESSAGE*)

'God is love... We love because he first loved us' (1 John 4:16b, 19).
'The fruit of the Spirit is love...' (Galatians 5:22). If we are God's
children, the fruit of the Spirit will be growing in us; day by day we'll
be showing the family likeness.

When the word 'love' is used in our English version of the New
Testament, it is in most, although not all, instances translating the
Greek word *agape*, or a word related to it. *Agape*-love is an unconditional gift-love, and is to be distinguished from erotic love,
parent–child love and friendship, for which there are different Greek
words. God loves us with *agape*-love, and Christians are to have
agape-love for one another.

Loving one another can't be left to those with a naturally affection-
ate or kindly disposition. Mutual tolerance may sound big-hearted by
the world's standards, but the New Testament makes no concessions
to those who find love too demanding. 'Love one another' is Jesus'
direct command to those who would follow him. And it comes with
an exacting standard: 'As I have loved you, so you must love one
another' (John 13:34).

An impossible ideal?

In giving this command to the disciples gathered in the upper room, was Jesus being hopelessly naïve—or cruelly unrealistic? Surely he knew them, their limitations, their tendency to squabble and jockey for position. And that was while he was there among them, as their undisputed leader! Relationships were bound to become more difficult once Jesus was no longer around to encourage good behaviour. To think of measuring our own behaviour by Christ's standard could seem even more unrealistic.

A command with a promise

Jesus' command to love one another comes at the start of his final briefing for the remaining eleven disciples. Judas has already left and will shortly betray Jesus into the hands of his accusers. Yes, things are about to get worse, but in the following chapter Jesus makes some weighty promises about not deserting them: he promises that the Holy Spirit will come and live in them, and that he himself will be with them in a new way.

If you love me, you will obey what I command. And I will ask the Father, and he will give you another Counsellor to be with you for ever—the Spirit of truth. The world cannot accept him, because it neither sees him nor knows him. But you know him, for he lives with you and will be in you. I will not leave you as orphans; I will come to you... you will realize that I am in my Father, and you are in me, and I am in you. (John 14:15–18, 20)

The command to love must not be divorced from the promise of the coming of the Holy Spirit. The third person of the Trinity is called the Counsellor, the *Paraclete* (more about this word in Chapter 5)— the one called alongside to help. The disciples will recognize him because they have already met him in Jesus.

It is significant that the command also comes with an assurance that obedience to Christ's teaching will allow the triune God to make his home with each disciple personally and individually. 'Whoever has my commands and obeys them, he is the one who loves me. He who loves me will be loved by my Father, and I too will love him and show myself to him… If anyone loves me, he will obey my teaching. My Father will love him, and we will come to him and make our home with him' (John 14:21, 23).

So, the command may have an impossible ring to it, but vast resources are available to those who set out to obey it. We can pray, 'God who is Love, come—be love in me.'

We are loved

We must resist any tendency to focus on the command and edit out the surrounding words which assure us that we are loved—and not just loved, but loved to an extent that is beyond our comprehension. For example, Jesus says: 'As the Father has loved me, so have I loved you. Now remain in my love' (John 15:9), before going on to say once again, 'My command is this: Love each other as I have loved you' (15:12).

When Paul urged the Ephesians to 'be full of love for others' (Ephesians 5:2, Living New Testament), he sandwiched the urging between reminders of the love God the Father has for his children and the love that prompted Christ's sacrifice of himself: 'Be imitators of God, therefore, as dearly loved children and live a life of love, just as Christ loved us and gave himself up for us as a fragrant offering and sacrifice to God' (Ephesians 5:1–2).

When we feel unloved, raw and vulnerable, we find it much harder to show consistent, generous-spirited, unconditional *agape*-love to those around us. Our capacity for loving is extended as we call to mind and revel in the never-ending, strong, sacrificial *agape*-love the Father has for us. 'How great is the love the Father has lavished on us, that we should be called children of God! And that is what we are!' (1 John 3:1). I'm told that the English 'how great' fails to do justice to the original Greek version!

God's love brings health to our inner being as he gives us a true perspective on ourselves. 'My dear children,' John continues, 'let's not just talk about love; let's practise real love. This is the only way we'll know we're living truly, living in God's reality. It's also the way to shut down debilitating self-criticism, even when there is something to it. For God is greater than our worried hearts and knows more about us than we do ourselves' (1 John 3:18–20, THE MESSAGE). God knows us better than we know ourselves—and he *still* loves us! Have you allowed this truth to sink deep into your soul?

Many women and men today feel unloved; some are unable to call to mind any experience of being loved. It's hardly surprising if such folk struggle with showing love to others. They may respond to attempts to show them love with suspicion or apparent disdain, but it's important not to give up on them. We can ask God to reveal ways in which they might be willing to receive love. Even those of us who are accustomed to being loved have different preferred ways of receiving love. For example, while some enjoy hearing loving words, others need to see love expressed in action. If a man or woman is suspicious of love, we can show them healthy *agape*-love enriching our own lives and the body of Christ more generally. We can pray for opportunities to serve them in love. We can pray for them to 'thaw'. We may also need to pray for patience—thawing takes time!

The 'root command'

'Remember the root command: Love one another' (John 15:17, THE MESSAGE). Jesus was facing the cross. Time was running out. None the less, he repeated himself: 'Love one another,' he told them— three times. Why is loving one another the 'root command'? Jesus gave us one of the reasons: 'By this all men will know that you are my disciples, if you love one another' (John 13:35). *Agape*-love is a distinctive mark of belonging to Christ.

The distinctive mark

In his first letter, John teaches that love for others is one of the two markers clearly distinguishing those who are children of God from those who are not: 'The one who won't practise righteous ways isn't from God, nor is the one who won't love brother or sister. A simple test' (1 John 3:10, THE MESSAGE). 'My beloved friends,' he pleads, 'let us continue to love each other since love comes from God.' He goes on:

The person who refuses to love doesn't know the first thing about God, because God is love—so you can't know him if you don't love… God is love. When we take up permanent residence in a life of love, we live in God and God lives in us… If anyone boasts, 'I love God,' and goes right on hating his brother or sister, thinking nothing of it, he is a liar. If he won't love the person he can see, how can he love the God he can't see? The command we have from Christ is blunt: Loving God includes loving people. You've got to love both. (1 John 4:7–8, 16b, 20–21, THE MESSAGE)

Church tradition has it that towards the end of the first century the elderly apostle John, so frail that he had to be carried to meet with his fellow Christians, said little other than 'Love one another, love one another'. Just as Jesus emphasized loving one another in the final hours before he was taken prisoner, it appears that John devoted much of his strength in his latter years to speaking and dictating letters about loving one another.

The call to love isn't confined to John's writings. 'Love one another as if your lives depended on it,' writes Peter (1 Peter 1:22; also 4:8, THE MESSAGE). It's a recurring feature of Paul's letters too, and the standard is no less exacting. For example, 'Love from the centre of who you are; don't fake it,' he urges the Romans (Romans 12:9, THE MESSAGE). To the Galatians he writes, 'The entire law is summed up in a single command: "Love your neighbour as yourself." If you keep on biting and devouring each other, watch out or you will be destroyed by each other' (Galatians 5:14–15). That last sentence is a graphic description of a painful reality in some churches today. We don't set out to bite and devour, it 'just happens'. Somehow things get out of hand, and small hurts lead to big hurts, and before you know it there's a painful mess and a divided fellowship.

Inclusive love

'May the Lord make your love increase and overflow for each other and for everyone else' (1 Thessalonians 3:12). I'm grateful that Paul mentions the divine resourcing of our love alongside this reference to its inclusivity. Jesus taught that we're not to confine our loving to those who will love us in return (Matthew 5:44–46). James makes a similar point: 'If you really keep the royal law found in Scripture, 'Love your neighbour as yourself,' you are doing right. But if you show favouritism, you sin and are convicted by the law as law-breakers' (James 2:8–9). If we are to keep the royal law, it appears that we can't be selective about whom we will love.

Agape-love shown to our brothers and sisters in Christ will over-flow naturally to those outside the body of Christ, because that's the nature of *agape*-love: it's a freely offered gift-love, open to all. It cannot lead to cliquishness and exclusivity: true *agape*-love is far too generous-spirited for that! The importance of this wider dimension of our loving is brought out by Richard Foster in his book *Freedom of Simplicity* (Triangle/SPCK, 1981). He repeats some contemporary writers' comments on the early Church: 'Julian the apostate, an enemy of Christianity, admitted that "the godless Galileans fed not only their [poor] but ours also". Tertullian wrote that the Christians' deeds of love were so noble that the pagan world confessed in astonishment, "See how they love one another."'

Foster emphasizes that these charitable acts 'grew out of a deep commitment to Christ and his call to care for the needy'. There is no suggestion that they were a ploy to make people think more highly of the Church, or that their purpose was to create openings for evangelism. The early Christians' loving actions simply reflected their hearts, which were overflowing with the love of Jesus. Two thousand years later, those around us have every right to expect God's message of love to be lived out by the body of Christ rather than simply preached.

Jean Vanier, founder of L'Arche community, is at pains to emphasize that the manner in which actions are performed contributes to the message received: 'To love is to *reveal* to a person that she or he is unique, special and worthy of attention. We reveal to another person his/her beauty and value not so much by words as by *the way* we look at, speak to, care for them and respond to their cry' (*Communities of Hope*, edited by Russell Bowman-Eadie and Graham Dodds, DLT, 1998). *Agape*-loving actions are a world away from the impersonal conveyor-belt type of 'charity' dished out at arm's length from behind a protective counter.

To men and women for whom the novelty of individualism and independence has begun to wear a bit thin, and whose present hunger is for connectedness and belonging, an outward-looking, loving community of God's people will speak volumes. What's more, where there's a living, breathing visual aid, evangelism and outreach will have less of the feel of cajoling a cold, damp engine on a winter morning. It'll be more like jumping on to a moving vehicle! Where the body of Christ is functioning as God intends, the members united in purpose because of their connection to the Head, and together revealing the character of Christ to the world, those outside will want to know more. Authentic Christ-likeness is still attractive to many, even in our cynical times.

Love in action

Paul knew that in the new churches it would be the day-to-day lives of the believers that would undergird—or undermine—the preaching and teaching. Just as he rejoiced to see growth in faith among his scattered congregations, he rejoiced also to see growth in love. It's among the first things he mentions in one of his letters to the Thessalonians: 'We ought always to thank God for you, brothers, and rightly so, because your faith is growing more and more, and the love every one of you has for each other is increasing' (2 Thessalonians 1:3).

So, what does 'agape-love in action' look like? Paul writes to the Romans that 'love must be sincere' (Romans 12:9). The Greek word translated 'sincere' means 'without pretence or hypocrisy'. There needs to be a consistency uniting the outward, visible actions and the inner life. Truly loving actions spring from loving hearts burgeoning with the fruit of the Spirit. (We'll be looking at the subject of showing love through serving in the next chapter.)

Speaking the truth in love

From time to time, hard things need to be said as part of showing genuine love. They are best said by those whose love is shown regularly in other less painful ways and so is not in doubt! Just as parents sometimes have to tell their children things they have no wish to hear, so within the Church, love has to be tough as well as tender. A key factor in the outcome will be the recipient's willingness to hear truth from God, however painful, in order to make progress in the Christian life. This of course presupposes that what is being said 'in love' is both true and from God—which is not always the case.

In their context, Paul's words about 'speaking the truth in love' (Ephesians 4:15) stand in contrast to what he has just said about immature Christians being vulnerable to deception by the latest new teaching put about by unscrupulous men (4:14). What follows is about growing up into Christ the Head, and playing a full part in the growing body of Christ (4:15–16). The context is important. From this, and from what New Testament scholars have to say, it would seem that the 'truth' here is more likely to be doctrinal in nature than the unpalatable 'home truths' with which the verse has become associated.

Several translations taken together will reveal more of what Paul was trying to convey. For example, 'Rather, let our lives lovingly express truth in all things—speaking truly, dealing truly, living truly.

Enfolded in love, let us grow up in every way and in all things into him, who is the Head' (Ephesians 4:15, Amplified Bible). Eugene Peterson reflects the meaning like this: 'God wants us to grow up, to know the whole truth and tell it in love—like Christ in everything. We take our lead from Christ, who is the source of everything we do' (4:15, THE MESSAGE).

Whatever Paul's original intentions in writing about 'speaking the truth in love', can we not find encouraging, affirming truths which could be spoken in love? For example: 'You were definitely the right person for that job—you've done it so well!' or, 'I'm so glad you dropped in. Your visit has lifted our spirits at a difficult time. Thank you.' Paul begins many of his letters with an encouraging truth. He writes to the Romans, 'I thank my God through Jesus Christ for all of you, because your faith is being reported all over the world' (Romans 1:8). There are plenty of other examples. Here are a couple: 'I thank my God every time I remember you. In all my prayers for all of you, I always pray with joy because of your partnership in the gospel' (Philippians 1:3–5); 'We always thank God, the Father of our Lord Jesus Christ, when we pray for you, because we have heard of your faith in Christ Jesus and of the love you have for all the saints' (Colossians 1:3–4). Can we follow Paul's example in our dealings with our brothers and sisters in Christ?

Christ in us

To summarize, the simplest answer to the question 'What does *agape*-love in action look like?' is that it looks like Jesus. If we're at a loss to know how to show love in a particular situation, we can ask ourselves, 'What would Jesus do?' However, while this may be a useful tactic in a crisis, it's insufficient as a rule for life. Philosopher and theologian Dallas Willard has written about the danger of assuming that all we need to do to 'follow Jesus' in a given situation is 'to try to behave as he did when he was "on the spot", under pressure or persecution or in the spotlight.' Willard continues:

There is no realization that what [Jesus] did in such cases was, in large and essential measure, the natural outflow of the life he lived when not on the spot. Asking ourselves 'What would Jesus do?' when suddenly in the face of an important situation simply is not an adequate discipline or preparation to enable one to live as he lived.

Willard stresses that we need 'to learn from Christ how to live our total lives, how to invest all our time and our energies of mind and body as he did. We must learn how to follow his preparations, the disciplines for life in God's rule that enabled him to receive his Father's constant and effective support while doing his will' (Dallas Willard, *The Spirit of the Disciplines*, Hodder and Stoughton, 1996).

If we are moved to pray that we'll increasingly have the mind of Christ, and that we'll know his character being formed in us by the ministry of the Holy Spirit, we must be prepared to accept the inevitable consequences: our lives will never be the same again. If we are to welcome 'Christ in us', some things (lots of things?) might have to go. The mind and character of Christ cannot be switched on for emergencies only; they can be formed in us, but not picked up and put down at will. Are we ready to welcome his character and his pattern of life?

Another answer to the question 'What does *agape*-love in action look like?' could be that it looks like the body of Christ described in the New Testament. As Christians, we're called not just to live individual Christ-like lives but to incarnate Christ corporately. We'll be exploring what this means in the remaining chapters of this book. But before we do so, let's take time to look at a very effective way of showing love: listening.

Listening to one another

'It's good to talk! Thanks for listening. See you again soon.' Never has it been so easy to keep in touch. But communication is more than words, and frequent exchanges using mobile phone text messages and e-mails may be giving a false impression. Indeed, if technology is being used habitually to escape face-to-face interaction, relational skills suffer. I fear the advent of a future generation whose members have an enviable typing speed but who rapidly become tongue-tied when obliged to make conversation. If they sit for hours in computer booths, clicking away, communicating electronically, they'll need a lot of help with learning to listen to one another!

With listening, as with most things in life, some folk have greater natural aptitude than others. However, I do believe that everyone can learn to listen more effectively if they want to do so, even if there are some who will never find it particularly easy. Becoming more aware of what's happening as we listen is a good place to start, and this is covered in the rest of the chapter. The Appendix on listening skills (page 154) takes the matter further, for those who would like to pursue it.

The act of listening

The very act of listening conveys a different message, depending on how it's done. Attentive listening can show love, respect, acceptance of a person's value and a concern to understand what's important to them. We may not agree with all that's being said (and may have to follow that up in due course), but we can still listen attentively. Listening isn't about agreeing or disagreeing, any more than it's a matter of solving problems or giving advice. Neither is listening the same as counselling. Listening is listening! It's about valuing someone as a person made in the image of God, and giving them the gift of our time and attention. What's more, if we've listened well, any contribution we do go on to make is likely to be not only of greater value but also more welcome.

Since time immemorial it has been recognized that 'just listening' helps others to think aloud, to hear themselves, to clarify things. Under the heading 'The Ministry of Listening', Dietrich Bonhoeffer wrote, more than half a century ago:

Secular education today is aware that often a person can be helped merely by having someone who will listen to him seriously, and upon this insight it has constructed its own soul therapy, which has attracted great numbers of people, including Christians. But Christians have forgotten that the ministry of listening has been committed to them by him who is himself the great listener and whose work they should share. We should listen with the ears of God that we may speak the Word of God.

DIETRICH BONHOEFFER, *LIFE TOGETHER*, SCM PRESS, 1954

Listening—or not listening?

'Are you receiving me? Over.' Sometimes it becomes increasingly obvious that the person we thought was listening to us has drifted to another wavelength. In our family, we have been known to say 'Earth to [person's name]. Come in, please.' Communicating with someone on a different planet is pretty frustrating!

It may be just a matter of tiredness or a temporary distraction, but if *not*-listening becomes the normal state of affairs we'll find it very painful. If those who say they love us, or who protest that they have our interests at heart, fail to listen when we try to communicate about things that matter to us, we'll soon start to doubt their sincerity. Our relationship will be affected. If our sense of our own worth is shaky, that too may suffer: we may tell ourselves that we're not worth listening to, or that it's all our fault for bothering them.

We need to learn both to listen and to show that we're listening. In this regard, even quite tiny actions speak louder than many words. The obstetrician who cared for me during my second pregnancy was an expert listener. In reality he worked very fast, but while he was with a patient his demeanour gave the impression that he had all the time in the world. He put patients at their ease, so they were able to express their concerns more easily. Doctors and others who sail in, exuding non-verbal messages about not wasting a second of their valuable time, are more likely to be faced with stuttering folk who've forgotten what they wanted to say.

Good listeners tend to have a certain composure which reflects an ability to cultivate an inner stillness. That's not to imply that they live untroubled lives without concerns or pressing needs—merely that they know how to put these to one side temporarily in order to give someone else's priorities their full attention. Telephone answering machines are a mixed blessing, but I always use mine to avoid interruptions when seeing people for spiritual direction. In addition, I often put it on when friends drop round, or when we're trying to give full attention to one another within the family. Friends and family members deserve good listening as well!

Going on hearing

It's true that some people abuse willing listeners by going over and over the same ground, without really wanting to break out of their rut. In a counselling relationship, a client's apparent reluctance to move on will be confronted when the time seems right, and sometimes it's necessary to do this within a friendship, too. But it's important not to be hasty or judgmental: listening may still have value, even when what is being said today is the same as yesterday and the day before. This is particularly true of those who are in the early stages of grief or shock. They may find it necessary to cover the same ground repetitively until they're ready to move on.

In chronically difficult circumstances in which, after all options have been explored, there genuinely is little prospect of change, simply being heard by fellow human beings may increase a struggler's ability to cope. Their isolation is reduced. Their sense of their own worth is more likely to be maintained. Being able to express the same old daily frustrations from time to time may prevent an explosive build-up. Explaining to someone else may help with getting everything in perspective.

When someone is disturbed or confused, we can support them and show love by going on saying, 'I hear you', even when we can't say, 'I understand'. I hope that if I live to a ripe old age and begin to ramble, I won't be obliged to talk only to myself! I hope there will be those who will remember the 'root command' to love, and allow

God to fill them with his love so that it can overflow to me as they listen.

Listening to the silence

Good listeners know that silences are to be heard rather than filled with chatter. A silence may represent a struggle to put complex thoughts or emotions into words, or a degree of fear or embarrassment: 'Will the person listening cope with hearing what I'm about to say?' In the latter case, a gentle word of reassurance may be necessary, to encourage the speaker to take the plunge. We can only fully hear those who choose to speak. In the absence of speech we may make a guess, but only a guess, at the meaning of the silence—pain, guilt, angry withdrawal, frustration at previous failure to hear, lack of trust in the hearer? We may also pray for supernatural wisdom and discernment.

In the midst of much chatter, we may detect the silence of omission: a subject has been skirted round or avoided in a way that feels odd. For example, the local news has carried a story about the sudden closure of the factory where George, a member of your house group, has worked for more than thirty years. When, during the next group meeting, the time comes to share concerns for prayer, George directs everyone's attention to a recent broadcast about the plight of flood victims in Asia, and says nothing at all about his job. You'd thought it odd when he arrived too late for the usual chatting over coffee before the meeting, but now you know that something's wrong. How you proceed will depend on many things, such as your knowledge of how George 'ticks', your own relationship with him, and the way the group has functioned in the past. All the signs are that George is still in shock. A gentle enquiry after the meeting might be all that he's able to cope with right now. The best response is to pray silently for wisdom—there's no automatic route to follow in this sort of situation.

A different sort of silence sometimes follows a time in which I've prayed and laid hands on someone. This is a silence in which God is at work. I try to let the person I've prayed for be the judge of when this silence has finished. They will often sit very still, and I aim to keep quiet until they're ready to move on.

Wise, loving listening

Before leaving the subject of listening, let me sound some warning bells. Listening to troubled folk is a wonderful way of showing love but, if they subsequently discover that their confidences have been betrayed, their overriding sense will be of violation.

Breaking a confidence is justified on rare occasions—for example, if there's a clear risk to someone's life, or if a child is being harmed. If at all possible, it's best to persuade the person to disclose the crisis themselves, to a doctor or another professional, or to obtain their agreement before you do so. If anyone ever asks you to promise that you won't tell anyone what they're about to tell you, it's best to think carefully what you might be getting yourself into. You could reply that, although you will do all you can to honour their confidence, you can't give an absolute promise because you have their well-being at heart.

'Keeping confidentiality' means not repeating or even hinting at what has been shared in confidence. Sharing confidential information 'for prayer' still counts as breaking a confidence, even if the person's name isn't used. If you know you find keeping confidences difficult, discourage people from confiding in you!

Boundaries

Loving one another doesn't mean being without boundaries. It's good to acknowledge our connectedness within the body of Christ, but boundaries of involvement are also appropriate, lest we become like Martha—drained with much helping and serving (Luke 10:40–42).

For example, it's important to know who sleeps in which house! If someone we've been listening to through a difficult time has gradually become a permanent fixture on our sofa and is increasingly reluctant to go home at night, we need to review what's been happening. Some people have a ministry of sharing their homes with troubled individuals, and that's great provided they have the capacity and the gifting necessary for this demanding role. It should be a calling, following the Lord's leading, not a consequence of it being difficult to get rid of uninvited 'lodgers'. Those involved should have their own support structures and, for the safety of all concerned, it's best to have some sort of accountability built in, too—however godly and *agape*-loving the home-sharers may be.

It's not easy to set new boundaries in established relationships, so it's wise to include them from the beginning. Sharing confidences even over a relatively short period of time increases intimacy. Sexual attraction can develop between highly unlikely candidates. Christians have a tendency to believe that 'it couldn't happen to me', but we're in a spiritual battle and the Enemy fights dirty. Other than in the short-term (by which I mean minutes, not months), showing love and acceptance through listening is best done by a person of the same sex, although even that does not exclude the possibility of unhealthy developments, especially if the listener is also a troubled person in need of love. The intimacy may be non-sexual but still inappropriate. For example, extreme closeness may be disrupting other relationships—the troubled person's or the listener's—or creating dependency. Indeed, any listening relationship that regularly intrudes on other relationships is questionable.

A good test is to ask yourself, 'How would I feel if the person concerned began confiding in someone else?' Then take time to examine the feelings that come up. (Jealousy? Relief?) Do these feelings suggest that boundaries have been or are in danger of being crossed? Sharing the listening role with a third person sounds cumbersome, and in the short term it may be impractical, but it reduces the risks associated with intimacy as well as providing additional support for all involved. If a person is particularly needy, it's usually better for everyone if they are cared for by several people working as a team rather than by one person on their own.

Time boundaries are mutually beneficial. Agreeing when to meet is usually better than saying 'do drop in any time', because the person being listened to then knows you've offered your full attention; they won't have to worry about whether or not they've interrupted something. 'Dropping in' can be a safety valve, but it may also foster dependency. Likewise, phoning for a chat when things are difficult can be a channel for encouragement and prayer, but if it becomes a knee-jerk reaction—a *substitute* for thinking and praying things through—this is counter-productive.

A less obvious boundary is that, whenever possible, people—even deeply troubled people—should speak for themselves. It's usually unwise and counter-productive to act as a go-between, speaking on behalf of someone else to their friend, mother-in-law, employer, church leader or estranged spouse about difficulties or concerns. If there is anxiety, you can always agree to being present in a supportive role. It may be necessary for you to set up the first contact if the relationship has broken down completely, but take steps to avoid becoming the channel for all communication. If the problem is long-standing and positions are entrenched, it may be best to enlist the help of a trained counsellor or professional mediator. You can then confine your listening to the person with whom you began, hearing their side of the problem rather than trying to cope with both.

If, while reading this, you've become concerned that one of your existing relationships is in difficulties, don't panic and run! Talk to the person concerned. Explain the need to move to team support, as described above. If the other person is unwilling to allow additional input, new boundaries must be established to limit the potential for problems. You may have to plan towards bringing the relationship to a close, perhaps with the assistance of your church leadership and the arrangement of suitable pastoral care and ongoing oversight. This sounds drastic, even 'unloving', but in my experience those who continue to try to soldier on alone, especially when a relationship is already unhealthy because of lack of boundaries, only get deeper into the mire. As a result, the person who is struggling may be damaged rather than helped.

Centred on God

When all is said and done, and all the necessary skills have been learned, practised and refined, the person we are and where we choose to keep our primary focus will have the greatest impact on those we meet. Canon Anne Long expresses this powerfully:

Ultimately, however skilled we may be, it is this grace, Christ at the centre, which really matters. Not that this undercuts the need for training but it is a reminder that finding our centre in God and being constantly drawn back to him, as surely as the compass needle is to its north pole, is what really counts. The prayerful life is not one in which we say frequent prayers but one in which nothing is done, said or listened to independently of God, so that all we are is permeated by him... Above all, the Christian listener is to be a 'living reminder' of God and one whose whole life incarnates the gifts and graces of Christ.

ANNE LONG, LISTENING, DAYBREAK/DLT, 1990

As Paul wrote to the Corinthians, 'No matter what I say, what I believe, and what I do, I'm bankrupt without love' (1 Corinthians 13:3, THE MESSAGE). 'Bankrupt without love' is the title of Study Session 3 (page 177).

It's great to spend time working at being a better listener. But we also need to spend time drinking in the love God has for us, receiving deep into our being the truth that his love for us—for me—is wider, longer, deeper and higher than can be imagined (Ephesians 3:17–19), and being drawn closer to Christ. That way, we'll truly know ourselves to be loved, and be able to share his love with others too.

Focus Point

- 'As the Father has loved me, so have I loved you' (John 15:9). Am I able to receive these words, which Jesus spoke to his first disciples, as an expression of how much Jesus loves *me*, or do I struggle with knowing that I am loved? You could use Paul's prayer for the Ephesians (Ephesians 3:16–21), inserting 'I' instead of 'you'. For example, 'I pray that I, being rooted and established in love...'
- The standard set by Jesus for our love for others could not be higher: 'As I have loved you, so you must love one another.' He goes on to say, 'By this all men will know that you are my disciples, if you love one another' (John 13:34–35). How do I feel when I read these words? If you become aware of shortcomings, take time to come to the Father in confession and repentance, and receive his forgiveness (1 John 1:9; 4:10).
- 'The command... is blunt: Loving God includes loving people. You've got to love both' (1 John 4:21, THE MESSAGE). Do I know someone who is prickly and seems to find it difficult to receive love? Am I ready to pray for them to 'thaw'—and to show them consistent love while they do? If so, ask God to show you the best way to show them *agape*-love.
- Think of someone you regard as a good listener. What is it about them that makes you think of them in this way?

Further reading

Christine Leonard, *Affirming Love*, BRF, 1999.
John 13:34–15:17; 1 John.

4

Serving

Serve one another in love.

GALATIANS 5:13

Each one should use whatever gift he has received to serve
others, faithfully administering God's grace in its various forms.

1 PETER 4:10

Imagine the scene: the disciples were gathered in the borrowed upper
room to eat the Jewish Passover meal, in accordance with their tradition. The meal was being served; the familiar pattern was unfolding.
Then something unexpected and unnerving happened...

The Servant King

The previous week had passed in a whirlwind of confusion. Jesus had
been keeping out of the public eye, because the chief priests and the
Pharisees were openly seeking to arrest him (John 11:53–57). But
after being anointed by Mary at Bethany (12:3) he'd entered Jerusalem in broad daylight, riding on a young donkey. The crowds
amassed in the city for the feast had come out to meet him. What a
fuss they'd made! Jesus hadn't seemed to mind, even when they'd
treated him like royalty! (12:12–13).

While the Passover meal was being served, Jesus took everyone by
surprise. He got up, removed his outer clothing, and took on the role
of the lowest of the low—a slave. Equipped with a bowl of water and

a towel, he went round washing all the disciples' feet. Peter watched, dumbfounded. He couldn't allow Jesus to wash *his* feet—it should have been the other way round. He'd have been honoured to wash his master's feet—not that he'd offered, of course; perhaps in retrospect this seemed an important oversight. There'd been no one whose job it was to do it, so they'd done without.

Setting an example

When Jesus returned to his place at the table, he asked them, 'Do you understand what I have done for you?' (John 13:12). If they did understand, their reply isn't recorded. Jesus' words to Peter explaining why he needed his feet—but only his feet—washed (13:10) have been taken to show that this was an acted parable, which some have linked with the ceremonial cleansing of the priests before they served God in the Temple (Exodus 40:30–32). Whether or not this was the case, we need to see the significance of Jesus' actions as multi-faceted.

The washing of the disciples' feet by Jesus pointed towards a cleansing from sin that he alone could bring. There were reasons why Peter had to let Jesus wash his feet, however uncomfortable he was with the idea. But alongside that was the explicit take-home message: this is what you are to do for one another (John 13:14–15). Generations of Christians have puzzled over what this might mean in practice. A few, taking the most literal interpretation, have even incorporated regular times of ceremonial foot-washing in their meetings.

In looking for Old Testament allusions, complex interpretations and 'obvious' responses, it's vital that we don't neglect Jesus' own answer to his question about what he had done: 'I have set you an example' (John 13:15). Study Session 4 (page 178) encourages reflection on what this might mean for us today.

John introduces his account of the foot-washing by saying this: 'Jesus... now showed them the full extent of his love' (13:1) or 'he loved them to the end' (RSV). This is a rich phrase, perhaps intentionally pointing forward from the foot-washing to Jesus' supreme act of love, his death for us on the cross. What stirs in your heart as you read it?

John closes his account by recording Jesus' words about status: 'No servant is greater than his master, nor is a messenger greater than the one who sent him' (13:16). The implication is clear: if Jesus their Lord and Master had been moved by *agape*-love to undertake a task which most ordinary people, the disciples included, would have regarded as beneath them, following Jesus was going to involve putting love before everything—before dignity, status, ideas about 'the way things are'. If the one whom they rightly called 'Lord' could do it, so could they.

Service in the New Testament

Paul's letter to the Romans refers to a gift of serving (Romans 12:7) but he makes it abundantly clear that all are called to serve—just as all are called to love. He urged the Galatians to 'serve [*douleuo*] one another in love', adding that 'the entire law is summed up in a single command: "Love your neighbour as yourself"' (Galatians 5:13–14). Note that Paul's words echo Jesus' summary of the Law (Luke 10:27).

Serving as a slave

Vine's Dictionary is a great help in exploring the New Testament usage of Greek words. Vine says that *doulos*, meaning 'slave' or 'bondman/maid' (from a verb meaning 'to bind'), 'originally the lowest term in the scale of servitude, came also to mean "one who gives himself up to the will of another"' (*Vine's Complete Expository Dictionary of Old and New Testament Words*, W.E. Vine, Merrill F. Unger, William White Jr, Thomas Nelson, Inc., 1985). We can give ourselves up to the will of another in a negative sense, as in being a 'slave to sin' (Romans 6:20), but Paul is using it positively when he describes himself as a 'servant [bondslave] of Jesus Christ' (Romans 1:1).

A commitment to serving one another is likely to take us out of our comfort zone, and we may, out of love, choose to do things we find unpleasant or frankly terrifying. But true *agape*-love, unconditional and self-giving as it is, does have limits. These are set by the fact that our primary calling is to be servants of Jesus Christ. There should never be any doubt that he alone is entitled to take centre place in our lives; he is Lord, and it is to his will that we commit ourselves. Showing love by serving one another should never take us outside the boundaries set for us by Jesus our Master.

Wisdom is needed to discern which boundaries may be extended and which are immovable—which are self-imposed on account of our preference for dignity or our desire to stay in control, and which have been set for us by God. God-ordained boundaries may come in the form of generally applicable commands, such as 'Do not commit adultery', or may be specific to us or to our situation as it is today. As individuals we may find this discernment difficult, but that's where being part of the body of Christ comes in, as I'll mention later.

Service and ministry

Our English word 'deacon' comes from the New Testament word *diakonos*, which is used both of domestic servants and of men (and one woman, Phoebe, Romans 16:1) with spiritual ministries. A related word, *diakonia*, is translated 'ministry', for example when speaking about the ministry of the Holy Spirit (2 Corinthians 3:8), and the ministry (KJV; or works of service, NIV) for which *all* God's people—women as well as men—are to be prepared (Ephesians 4:12). *Diakonos/diakonia* is by far the most common way of referring to Christian ministry in the New Testament.

Interestingly, similar Greek words are used not only for the waiting at table for which the seven 'deacons' were appointed, but also for the ministry of the word into which the Twelve were thereby released (Acts 6:1–6). Words from the same root are used for Martha's serving at Bethany (John 12:2), and 'the task [ministry] of testifying to the gospel of God's grace' entrusted by Christ to the apostle Paul (Acts

20:24; see also numerous similar references, for example, 2 Corinthians 3:6, 1 Thessalonians 3:2).

A church leader today may be called a 'minister', which comes from the Latin for 'servant'. This is related to the familiar Latin word *minus*, meaning 'less'. In New Testament times, every church member was a 'minister', just as everyone—leaders included—was part of the 'laity', the people of God (*laos*; see, for example, Hebrews 4:9; 1 Peter 2:9. For a full explanation, refer to R. Paul Stevens, *The Abolition of the Laity: Vocation, Work and Ministry in a Biblical Perspective*, Paternoster Press, 2000).

Serving in today's Church

'There are different kinds of service,' wrote Paul to the Corinthians, 'but the same Lord' (1 Corinthians 12:5). I wonder if Paul was writing to Christians in a similar situation to our own, in which certain kinds of service are dignified with the term 'ministry' and are seen as important, while others are not? Stevens notes:

William Tyndale, the English reformer, was considered heretical and executed for teaching, among other things, that 'there is no work better than another to please God: to pour water, to wash dishes, to be a souter [cobbler], or an apostle, all are one; to wash dishes and to preach are all one, as touching the deed, to please God'.
THE ABOLITION OF THE LAITY

The New Testament knows nothing of our service/ministry hierarchies. Neither does it portray a body of Christ in which the greater part is paralysed or flaccid while a small section rushes around trying to do all the work—a consequence of the hierarchical approach. If we are to take seriously the New Testament model for Christian service, we have to resist any tendency to assign value to people and their actions according to the world's rankings. They count for nothing in the Kingdom of God.

Valued by God, his people and the community

Our parish has for many years benefited from the faithful behind-the-scenes service of Phyllis, who, with her army of helpers, has kept our main church and hall swept, polished and mended. Pat and his wife, Win, have fulfilled a similar role in the small daughter church. Every church family needs those with practical serving gifts like Phyllis, Pat, Win and their helpers—and plenty more besides.

A different Pat has taken a short course in footcare. She uses the skills gained to help local elderly people who find it difficult to cut their own toenails. Those who enjoy visiting elderly, housebound folk used to think that everyone found it as delightful and easy as they do! Now some of them belong to the church Visiting Team whose members, while invisible to most of us, are the body of Christ in loving action to those who through illness or advancing years are temporarily or permanently out of circulation. Another often-unseen helper is Peter. His readiness to turn up with his van to move a second-hand refrigerator or bed to those in need of them, or to assist with moving house, has made a valuable contribution to the church's pastoral care.

Our team of technophiles sets up and mans the church microphone system, which comes into prominence only on the odd occasion when it goes wrong. And they get around, too, in spite of the fact that packing up the system to transport it to outside events is no trivial task. Charlie has built a large movable barbecue, and can be relied on to produce a great feast—for church members, for an outreach event… well, for anyone or anything, really! Although many of our events involve 'bring and share' catering, which means everyone turning up with something to share with everyone else, we're blessed with very capable cooks who can rustle up a breakfast, lunch or supper for a crowd without appearing to turn a hair. I could go on…

The individuals and teams mentioned would probably tell you that they're just doing what they can to help—doing what they're good at. So why am I labouring the point by telling you about them? First, to emphasize that serving includes more than cleaning church buildings and making cups of tea; and second, to draw attention to the fact that these practical gifts have spiritual significance, and are an indispensable part of the church's interaction with the wider community.

Does what they do have 'spiritual significance'? Of course it does! These dear brothers and sisters are, by their actions, revealing the presence of Christ in the world—the presence of Christ in their lives. To put it in theological language, it's an aspect of 'incarnational reality'—'God with us' (Matthew 1:23). For far too long, much of the Christian Church has had a tendency to behave as if the best way to reveal Christ to others were through words. Much-needed practical and befriending gifts have lain dormant, because those to whom they've been given were never encouraged to see them as relevant or important, let alone 'spiritual'. Centuries ago, Francis of Assisi is said to have advised his fellow workers to 'preach the gospel at all times... and use words if you must'.

Lovingly serving Christ

As I've asked myself the question 'What is serving?' I've found it impossible to devise a brief definition that does justice to the diversity. The best I can do is to say that Christian service involves lovingly using God-given gifts and talents to meet individual and/or corporate needs, so building up the body of Christ and bringing glory to him. The defining feature of Christian service is that it is serving Christ. Beyond that, the variety is immense.

Peter's attempt at a summary is this: 'Each one should use whatever gift he has received to serve [*diakoneo*] others, faithfully administering God's grace in its various forms' (1 Peter 4:10). He had just written, 'Above all, love each other deeply, because love covers over a multitude of sins' (4:8)—an example of loving and serving being written about in close proximity.

The most striking juxtaposition of loving and serving is in Paul's first letter to the Corinthians. A block of teaching on serving and ministering using spiritual gifts is 'interrupted' by the great chapter on love. In the first few verses of this chapter Paul makes it clear that great things done in God's name are noisy nothingness if they are done without *agape*-love (1 Corinthians 13:1-3). It's easy to overlook the forcefulness of his words, especially if we know them well and enjoy the poetic language. In THE MESSAGE Eugene Peterson brings out the meaning as follows:

If I speak with human eloquence and angelic ecstasy but don't love, I'm nothing but the creaking of a rusty gate. If I speak God's Word with power, revealing all his mysteries and making everything plain as day, and if I have faith that says to a mountain, 'Jump,' and it jumps, but I don't love, I'm nothing. If I give everything I own to the poor and even go to the stake to be burned as a martyr, but I don't love, I've gotten nowhere. So, no matter what I say, what I believe, and what I do, I'm bankrupt without love.
(1 Corinthians 13:1-3)

Whatever version we read, the main point is painfully clear: love has to undergird and be a constant thread through all that we do. If *without love* we invite a lonely person to a meal, clear the confetti from the church doorway, or preach a carefully prepared sermon, there will be a sense in which the action counts for nothing.

Reflecting on motives and attitudes

In the seventeenth century, Brother Lawrence was a lay brother in a Carmelite community. He wrote that 'we ought not to be weary of doing little things for the love of God, who regards not the greatness of the work, but the love with which it is performed' (Brother Lawrence, *The Practice of the Presence of God*, Mowbray, 1914). God sees beyond our actions and into our hearts, where our attitudes may be hidden from others but not from him.

Mixed motives and ungodly attitudes are signs of our being not yet fully redeemed. Counselling, spiritual direction and mentoring are specialized relationships which offer a forum for healthy reflection, giving God space to speak into our lives. However, it's good to be aware that *morbid* reflection provides opportunities for the 'accuser of our brethren' (Revelation 12:10, RSV). Our motives matter, but once we start trying to analyse them, it's easy to end up tied in knots! 'Did I offer a lift to that woman because she needed one, or was I trying to impress others with my willingness to go the extra mile?' 'Did I agree to preach on Sunday in order to share God's word with his people, or because I get a real buzz out of preaching?'

Leanne Payne has described an obsessive tendency to pick life to pieces while living it, which she calls 'the disease of introspection' (*The Healing Presence*, Kingsway, 1990). Those of us who are by nature strongly reflective can guard against it by refusing to engage in interminable dialogues with ourselves over the exact details of our motivation. For me, the answer has been to stop analysing my motives and to ask God simply to show me anything that's in my heart of which I need to repent. Even for those who have never tied themselves in counter-productive knots while trying to explore their own motivation, this is still the best way to go about it.

Mixed motives and ungodly attitudes may also be signs of a brokenness that is crying out for healing. Some are driven to help others as a way of trying to feel better about themselves, using good deeds as an anaesthetic for their emotional pain. The 'receivers' are in fact serving the emotional needs of the helper. I have written at length about this in *Driven Beyond the Call of God*. If we see a sister or brother in Christ helping others in a way which has all the hallmarks of drivenness or addiction, we'll need to pray for wisdom to know how to respond. Their self-esteem is likely to be low, so we must take care not to crush it further.

Helping one another to discern God's will

Jenny, an artist, has used her art to bring glory to God and to enrich the life of her local church (and numerous other churches, too) in the years since she became a Christian. Jenny has also led worship and times of prayer, and has brought blessing to individuals and the church through serving in unseen ways as well. Nevertheless, for years Jenny felt that she was failing because, when she looked at the ways of serving described by Jesus in Matthew 25:35–36 (feeding the hungry, giving drink to the thirsty... visiting those in prison), she knew that she wasn't doing everything on the list. When Jenny attended our church's 'Bodybuilding Course', it was liberating for her to hear that, while the body of Christ is called to serve in a profusion of ways, only a limited number can be the calling of any one woman or man at any particular time. As a result of the teaching on the course, Jenny was able to lay down the false guilt that had been distracting her from what the Lord *had* been calling her to do.

Sometimes fellow Christians appear to be finding it difficult to discern God's will when the root problem is a reluctance to embrace his purposes for their lives. On one occasion when I was praying with someone who was seeking guidance, I felt led to stop and ask the person concerned if God had already told them to do something. They said that he had. My sense was that God was waiting for obedience on the first issue, whatever it was, before providing guidance on the issue that was their current concern; to him, the first issue was more important.

Even when we've set our hearts to follow Christ and we're anxious to be sensitive to the leading of the Holy Spirit, it's not always easy to be certain that we're hearing God aright. If we're prepared to share our dilemma with others in the body of Christ, they may be able to help us—by intercession, by listening prayer, by acting as a sounding board as we think things through, by wise and loving words born out of their knowledge of us and our 'blind spots', and so on. We can ask others to pray with us—both specifically that we'll be shown clearly whether or not God is wanting us to take on a particular role, and more generally that we'll have a clearer view of his direction for us. On occasions, others may be given clear insight concerning our situation, but we must be careful not to give ourselves over to their will rather than to God's, or to abdicate all responsibility for receiving God's guidance.

Obedient servants

Christ poured himself out, taking the form of a slave in humble obedience to the Father (Philippians 2:7–8), and we as his disciples are called to the same way of life. True humility is an unself-conscious virtue. We can get ourselves into a real muddle if we pursue it for its own sake. Those who turn down opportunities for serving the Lord in what they see as higher-profile ways because they fear they will be seen as lacking humility are missing the point.

It's vital to retain the same heart attitudes whether serving as monarch or shoe-shiner: we are the Lord's servants, and any glory goes to him (1 Peter 4:11). The emphasis must be on serving in the ways *God* has prepared for us (Ephesians 2:10). God is our Master, and he has the authority to ask us to do all manner of things. Given his great love for us, it's not surprising that he often asks us to do things we find pleasurable! Given that he made us and knows us through and through, he knows what we're good at and what we find difficult. He knows when it's time to move on from a familiar role to one in which our faith will receive greater exercise. He knows what we're ready for—even when we're sure he's got it wrong!—and what we can't handle just at the moment.

God looks for obedience rather than perfection

Men and women sometimes turn down opportunities for fruitful service because of a misguided perfectionism. Yes, we should be concerned to offer God the best we can give. We may be right that others would perform better than us but, if we're clearly being led by God (that is, the calling we are sensing is being confirmed by others) to have a go at something new, or to repeat something we didn't get right first time, isn't saying 'No' disobedience?

If we're in leadership, are we aware that a concern for God's name to be honoured by all that happens in the fellowship, or wanting to protect our flock from ministry by those who are as yet untried and untested, may be a cloak for this same perfectionistic attitude?

Leaders do well to avoid a cavalier approach to encouraging church members in new areas of service, but elevating the need for a 'perfect' end product above the importance of obeying God is always dangerous.

Of course I'm not saying that it's right to say 'Yes' to everything. It can be godly, kind and in every way right to say 'No'. It might, for example, be a matter of recognizing that God has prepared and equipped us for other tasks—not this one—or we may recognize that what a friend is asking us to do 'to help' will add to their problems rather than solve them. Some lack the freedom to say 'No' when appropriate to do so, because they've never learned to draw healthy boundaries between what is and what is not their responsibility. They may, for example, feel responsible for everyone's happiness and satisfaction—a terrible burden to bear as, however hard they try, they won't be able to make everyone happy.

An inability to say 'No' to the wrong things can go hand in hand with feelings of unworthiness which lead to turning down those opportunities which *are* God-given, saying, 'I'm not that clever', or 'That can't be for me.' Some are only willing to take on menial and unpleasant service, because they see themselves as of little value, or as only worthy of the jobs no one else wants. But as Frederick Buechner poetically puts it, 'Neither the hair shirt nor the soft berth will do. The place God calls you to is the place where your deep gladness and the world's deep hunger meet' (Frederick Buechner, *Wishful Thinking—A Seeker's ABC*, Mowbray, 1993).

Helping one another to choose obedience

We must set our sights on encouraging others in their obedience, rather than giving them permission to feel more comfortable with their disobedience. Nevertheless, it's worth noting that what God requires is obedience rather than compliance; the visible effects may be similar, but the heart-attitudes and the long-term consequences are very different. Systematic coercion may result in an acceptable quota of good works: some will comply out of fear; others merely out of a desire for a quiet life. But this is a long way from encouraging one another in a heartfelt obedience to God's perceived will, responding to his love with a desire to serve him faithfully.

We can help one another to choose obedience by remembering to follow things up—in conversation as well as in prayer: 'I've been praying about the opportunity/dilemma you mentioned. Have you arrived at a decision yet?' From time to time, in the context of spiritual direction, a brother or sister in Christ will tell me that they've been aware of the Lord leading in a particular direction but have not yet done anything about it. Sometimes they're helped by talking through the reasons for their hesitation, but it's important that the act of explaining the delay to me doesn't take the place of sorting things out with God. Has their hesitation been a matter of dis-obedience? If so, repentance is necessary. Is there a conflict between their will and God's will? How do they plan to resolve it? Or is it more a matter of neglect—the cares of the world taking priority? One of the greatest services we can render in love is to help our brothers and sisters in Christ to go on responding to his lordship, whatever the cost.

Focus Point

- Eugene Peterson's expression 'bankrupt without love' (see page 68; 1 Corinthians 13:3, *THE MESSAGE*) packs a powerful punch. Do I really believe it's that serious—that if I 'have not love' (NIV) my actions count for nothing?
- Do I have a problem with saying 'No' to the things which are not part of God's call for me—or with saying 'Yes' to the things that are?
- Do I have a tendency to focus on honouring God by doing things perfectly rather than on the importance of obedience?

*For we are God's workmanship
created in Christ Jesus to do good works,
which God prepared in advance for us to do.*

Learn this verse (Ephesians 2:10, NIV—or your preferred version) by heart, and ask God to help you to call it to mind as you go about your activities over the next week. See how each of its three parts influences your attitude to life in general, as well as to those areas you're already aware of as coming under the heading of Christian service.

Further reading

Luke 10:25–37; Philippians 2.

5

Encouraging and Comforting

Encourage one another daily.
HEBREWS 3:13

Praise be to the God and Father of our Lord Jesus Christ, the
Father of compassion and the God of all comfort, who comforts
us in all our troubles, so that we can comfort those in any
trouble with the comfort we ourselves have received from God.
2 CORINTHIANS 1:3–4

If you close your eyes and think of the word 'comfort', what pictures
come to mind? Do you know anybody whom you'd call a real
encourager?

Strong comfort!

In the New Testament, most of the references to encouragement
('exhortation' in the older versions) and comfort are translations of
the same word, *paraklesis*. We'll come closer to the sense of the Greek
if we allow for the fact that a verb from the same root as *paraklesis* is
sometimes translated 'appeal' or 'urge' (KJV, 'beseech'). For example,
Paul writes, 'I *appeal* to you, brothers, in the name of our Lord Jesus
Christ, that all of you agree with one another so that there may be no
divisions among you' (1 Corinthians 1:10); and 'I *urge* you, brothers,
in view of God's mercy, to offer your bodies as living sacrifices'
(Romans 12:1).

The Holy Spirit, the Comforter

Encouragement is part of the role of the Holy Spirit. Some commentators refer to him as 'the Paraclete', harking back to the Greek *parakletos*. A paraclete is literally 'one called alongside'. The sense is that help is on offer, such as from an advocate in a court of law.

In John's Gospel, a word from the same Greek root is in action when the Holy Spirit is called 'the Comforter' (John 14:26; 15:26; 16:7, KJV). When Jesus speaks of him as 'another Comforter' (John 14:16, KJV), he is saying 'another *of the same kind*'—that is, like Jesus himself. It's interesting to note that, according to Vine's Dictionary, the Holy Spirit's name '"Comforter"... corresponds to the name *"Menahem"*, given by the Hebrews to the Messiah'.

The comfort 'of the same kind' provided by Jesus and the Holy Spirit has little in common with media portrayals of comfort, such as hot chocolate drinks or armchairs by the fireside. It's more to do with galvanizing than soothing. Generally speaking, the New Testament concept of comfort and encouragement has a more solid, substantial and proactive feel to it than our modern usage of the English words conveys.

Just as the word 'comforter' has changed over the centuries, the NIV's rendering of the Holy Spirit's title as 'the Counsellor' has taken on a different slant more recently because of the popularization of the specialized helping ministry known as counselling. It's important to retain the broadness of 'one called alongside' (to help), and not to allow the drift in meaning to narrow the role of the Holy Spirit—or indeed to mislead us into thinking that only trained counsellors can encourage or comfort others within the body of Christ! It's also vital to remember that our own encouraging and comforting needs the empowering presence of 'the Paraclete', 'the Comforter', the Holy Spirit.

Receive it—and pass it on!

'We were harassed at every turn—conflicts on the outside, fears within,' wrote Paul. 'But God, who comforts the downcast, comforted us by the coming of Titus, and not only by his coming but also by the comfort you had given him' (2 Corinthians 7:5–7). Titus had been sent by God to comfort Paul, having already received comfort and encouragement from the Corinthians. There's an important principle at work here: receive it, and pass it on!

In addition to writing letters to be read out and passed around to encourage first-century believers, Paul made a point of sending personal messengers. To the Thessalonians he sent Timothy, to strengthen and encourage them in their faith, 'so that no one would be unsettled by these trials' (1 Thessalonians 3:3). Writing to the Ephesians from prison, Paul closed by saying that 'Tychicus, the dear brother and faithful servant in the Lord, will tell you everything, so that you also may know how I am and what I am doing. I am sending him to you for this very purpose, that you may know how we are, and that he may encourage you' (Ephesians 6:21–22). Tychicus is spoken of in similar vein in Paul's letter to the Colossians (Colossians 4:8).

Joseph, a Levite from Cyprus, is better known by the apostles' nickname for him—Barnabas, meaning 'Son of Encouragement' (Acts 4:36). He was powerfully used by God, acting as an instrument of transformation in Paul's life. While others were still wary, Barnabas accepted Paul's story of conversion to Christ and introduced him to the apostles (9:26–27). Some years later, Barnabas was the one who travelled to Tarsus to look for Paul, taking him to Antioch because there was much work to be done (11:25–26). So began their partnership in the gospel and Paul's ministry, which had a tremendous impact on the early Church and still blesses us today. We all owe a great debt to this 'Son of Encouragement'!

Paul received much encouragement and comfort from numerous brothers and sisters in Christ during his ministry, especially after he was imprisoned by the ruling authorities. Hearing that Paul and the soldiers guarding him would be arriving in Rome, brothers in Christ travelled a great distance—some more than fifty miles—in order to accompany him on the last part of his route. Paul had previously written of his hope that one day they might be able to meet and encourage each other (Romans 1:11–12). It is recorded that 'At the sight of these men Paul thanked God and was encouraged' (Acts

28:15). It's easy to imagine his delight at being greeted by those prepared to be known as his friends, especially at the end of such a long and eventful journey.

Biblical encouragement

So what in practical terms does the New Testament mean by 'encouragement'? (I'm just going to use the word 'encouragement' now, rather than 'comfort', as the same Greek word is used for both.) Biblical encouragement is directed towards an increase in fruit for the Kingdom, and continuing growth in the faith and spirituality of our sisters and brothers in Christ—not just a growth in morale. It comes in many forms, but for simplicity let's look at it under four headings: encouragement to live biblically, encouragement in sound doctrine, encouragement in faith and encouragement in prayer.

Encouragement to live biblically

A biblical lifestyle is intended to be a 24-hour, seven-days-a-week commitment for all Christians; we're all meant to be in full-time service. We can't take time off from being sanctified (made holy) when we go to work, or to a party with our mates. Our lifestyle is a powerful way of challenging those around us to consider Christ—so long as it's consistent with what we say we believe.

Most of us need all the help we can get with going on living as 'saints' ('holy ones', God's set-apart people). While a spiritual director who is seen from time to time may be of assistance, the body of Christ around us is ideally placed for ongoing support. 'Encourage one another daily,' says the writer to the Hebrews (Hebrews 3:13). We'll be more effective in encouraging and praying for others if we have some idea of the dilemmas they face: for example, any pressure—in the workplace or in relationships—to go against biblical standards. If the circumstances of the members of your home group or other small group are unknown to you, would you be happy to ask about them?

As part of encouraging one another to live biblically, our church began to use 'Called to Serve', a discipleship course published by Time Ministries International. We found that one of the recurring emphases was on applying the scriptures to daily life, and particularly to our relationships. For those of us who had been Christians for years, the major doctrinal aspects of the course were straightforward. However, the teaching on refraining from gossip, not harbouring resentment against one another, maintaining the unity of the Spirit, honouring leaders, not letting the sun go down on our wrath and so on, was much more of a shock to the system! Yes, we'd heard it all before, but had we really taken it on board? We tried to encourage one another to press on and to apply what we were learning—rather than just agreeing that it was difficult and sympathizing!

As has already been laid out in Chapter 4, a biblical lifestyle includes service to others—in the community as well as within God's family. How can we set about encouraging others with this aspect of biblical living? Encouraging words will be of value, but what about practical encouragement, such as babysitting or transport? Offering these aids will demonstrate that we see their service as valuable, worth supporting. We can also assure them of our prayers—provided, of course, that we do intend to pray! Some people will appreciate help with getting started in Christian service, perhaps by being given an opportunity to serve alongside us, warming to the task as the Holy Spirit touches their heart too. On the other hand, the Lord may be calling us to come alongside someone else, to share their burden of responsibility. Having recently seen television pictures of the Oxford and Cambridge teams preparing for the Boat Race, I'm mindful of shouting through a megaphone from a distance as a model for spurring on. But in some circumstances it's even more effective to climb into the same boat and pick up an oar.

Encouragement in sound doctrine

Paul, writing to Titus, told him that one of the functions of an elder was to 'hold firmly to the trustworthy message as it has been taught, so that he can encourage others by sound doctrine and refute those who oppose it' (Titus 1:9). We might suppose that the free availability in accessible language of copies of the gold standard for doctrine, the Bible, means that our need for encouragement in this area is less than that of the early Christians. Biblical preaching in church on Sundays should make a substantial contribution to people's understanding of doctrinal issues, but I wonder whether it really does in practice.

In conversation with some who have listened to biblical preaching for decades, I've found their understanding of basic doctrines to be surprisingly limited. In a few cases it would appear that their thinking has been so heavily influenced by popular culture and superstition that the Sunday preaching has passed them by. For example, the sovereignty of God is a difficult concept for someone whose expectations are controlled by a daily horoscope; and teaching on the uniqueness of Christ may fail to impact someone who has embraced the notion that it doesn't matter what you believe as long as you're sincere.

When we teach the 'Called to Serve' course, we use additional questions for group discussion and to test out informally whether or not individuals have grasped key points. After covering the subject of justification by faith, I used the following supplementary question: 'If you were to die tonight, how do you know that God would let you into heaven?' The participants divided into twos and threes to think through their answers, and then fed back to the group. It was noticeable that although they had all appeared to receive the doctrine with their minds, it had not necessarily brought assurance of a place in heaven.

In some cases, a failure to absorb Christian teaching may be a matter of a different preferred learning style. For too long the Church and much of our national education system has assumed that everyone learns in the same way. In fact, they don't. Some people absorb teaching more effectively in a relational setting, where interaction and questioning are expected and welcomed, while others learn best by getting involved with practical applications of what they're learning.

Those who enjoy lecture-style teaching may be less enthusiastic about small-group and practical learning but, if they can be persuaded to stick with it, they may be pleasantly surprised.

Doctrine isn't just for theologians to ponder—it's meant to make a difference to how we see life, and to be a resource from which to draw during our daily struggles. I have listened to far too many distraught Christians telling me that God couldn't possibly love them, and that the sin they have committed is too awful for him to forgive. Again and again I've found it necessary to remind sisters and brothers that when 'the Accuser' tells them that they're a no-good waste of space, or that they've really fouled up this time—'God's *never* going to forgive *that*!'—they're not supposed to agree with him! They should be able to recall that God has promised to forgive and cleanse his children when they come to him in confession and repentance. It's not simply a matter of memorizing key verses. We all need to know, in the fullest sense of heart-knowing, that we are children of God, saved by grace, who need fear no condemnation (John 1:12; Ephesians 2:8; Romans 8:1).

As trust is built up, we can help one another to check that our foundational beliefs are biblical. We can also gently challenge—or be challenged—if there seems to be a problem with applying the doctrines to everyday life. In the context of seeking peace in the midst of anxieties, Paul urged the Christians at Philippi to fill their minds with that which is true, noble, right, pure and so on (Philippians 4:8). Could we do more to encourage one another to allow God's truth to minister deep assurance to our souls, perhaps at the same time urging one another to absorb less of the untrue, ignoble, immoral and impure stuff that comes to us by way of television and the other media?

Encouragement in faith

'Faith is being sure of what we hope for and certain of what we do not see' (Hebrews 11:1). In contrast to the world's view of faith as a leap into the unknown with a fifty–fifty (or worse) chance of a safe landing, the biblical picture is of stepping out confidently with our eyes on Jesus, the one who has gone before us (12:1–3). Yet the reality is that, for many Christians, doubts outweigh certainties, and faith feels a bit like 'pinning the tail on the donkey'—desperate for a hit, fearful of a miss.

Encouraging one another in faith doesn't require doubts to be buried or for a brave face to be grafted on to lack of assurance; mutual encouragement will include help with areas of difficulty. Many Christians look back and say that their faith became noticeably stronger in a particularly trying period, when all the usual props had been knocked away. But how may we stimulate one another's faith in the quieter times? Sharing relevant scriptures and personal experiences will be of value, but the example we set by the long-term priorities we establish for our lives, our daily choices, and the way we handle our own crises and difficulties may speak even more loudly.

Above all, encouraging one another in faith involves reminding one another what God is like, what he has done and what he has promised to do. 'He who promised is faithful' (Hebrews 10:23). Ultimately, the fact that our faith is in a great God is more important than the quantity or strength of our faith, and that in itself is encouraging.

Encouragement in prayer

Uniting in prayer can be a means of mutual encouragement. News of answered prayer is heartening, especially for those who joined in the praying, and this builds faith, too. We can also help by reminding one another that God is good; he has told us to ask, and has promised that he will hear our prayers and give us 'good gifts' (Matthew 7:11). We can point one another to scripture passages telling of the confidence we may have when we approach God, and reminding us that 'if we ask anything according to his will, he hears us' (1 John 5:14). But let's also remind one another that prayer is meant to involve much more than asking for things.

Prayer has a central role in the growth and sustaining of our relationship with God. Spiritual directors give their directees' prayer life plenty of attention; some focus almost exclusively on it. Hymn writers and others, in trying to underline its essential nature, have likened praying to breathing, yet many Christians find it the most difficult aspect of their spirituality. I therefore make no apologies for writing at greater length about this aspect of encouraging one another.

Why does everyone seem to believe that everyone else is better at praying than they are? And why are many trying to pray in the way they feel they ought to pray, rather than making the most of the way or ways in which they can pray? It's good to explore the breadth of prayer, and to step outside our comfort zone, but that's best done as the Lord leads and not out of a spiritual inferiority complex! If we were all able to relax a little, and learn from the Holy Spirit and one another, the body of Christ would be greatly strengthened. Our backgrounds differ; our spiritual journeys have been diverse, even if we're currently worshipping together; our personalities are different and multi-faceted; our styles for everyday communications vary widely. Should we all expect to pray to our heavenly Father in the same way? Of course not!

Those who have been brought up in a Christian home will have learned ways of praying—a valuable foundation when getting started, but this may have inhibited a move to other forms of prayer later on. Some will have been brought up to pray after reading the Bible, which can be very productive, but it's good to have the freedom to do things differently. Others who have always moved straight to prayer might find that starting by meditating on a scripture passage brings a new dimension to their praying. Using a prayer from the Bible (for example, one of the psalms; Ephesians 3:14–21; Hebrews 13:20–21; Jude 24–25), may also be beneficial. I'm happy to pray out loud or silently, but in recent years I've written some of my prayers in a prayer journal—but then, I'm a writer! I know that some of my friends find the very idea of writing prayers totally paralyzing.

At various stages of my Christian life I've been spurred on in prayer by different brothers and sisters in Christ. Some have been friends; others I do not know personally, but they have written helpfully about deepening their walk with God through prayer. In recent years I've been encouraged in prayer by my friend Pam. Having had no contact with church at all, she became a Christian in her late thirties. 'Talk to God,' Pam was told, and so she did, using the same language and direct style as she would when talking to a friend. I remember one of the first times I heard Pam pray in a group. Her prayer about a particularly difficult situation began, 'Well, Jesus, it's like this…'. It wasn't long before Pam realized that not everyone else prays so freely. At times she has felt that she ought to pray 'proper prayers—like everyone else', but I and others have encouraged her to avoid an unnatural style of praying that would spoil her dialogue with God.

It's vital that we don't give new Christians the idea that their first stumbling efforts at prayer are in some way inadequate. Those who are parents will remember their delight at their child's first efforts at sentence-building. Was the grammar a little muddled? Were you the least bit bothered? In the same way, Father God delights to hear his children's prayers, however inelegantly composed. Author and pastoral counsellor Rosemary Green told me of her amazement that, after signing a 'decision card' many years ago at university, she was immediately invited to pray aloud, in her own words. She added: 'I stumbled through a prayer—and have evermore been grateful that I was encouraged to break the sound barrier of praying aloud right at the start.'

When ordinary words fail, some are able to give expression to their hearts by praying in tongues. Coming to the end of their ability to pray in words, some pray in pictures. In times of confusion and distress I used to find it a great pressure that I was unable to explain everything to God. But his hearing of our prayers is not limited by our ability to verbalize the cries of our hearts, as I learned from sisters and brothers in Christ who use wordless prayer. I began experimenting with this sort of prayer by praying 'Lord… you know', thanking him that I didn't have to explain. Since then I've been able to pray 'Lord… you know' with others as we've together brought complicated or seemingly impossible situations before God. 'God's Spirit is right alongside helping us along. If we don't know how or what to pray, it doesn't matter.

He does our praying in and for us, making prayer out of our wordless sighs, our aching groans' (Romans 8:26, *THE MESSAGE*).

Laying aside all matters of method, let's not forget that when God hears our prayers he inevitably hears so much more than our words. Words do have value: spoken words are useful in that they enable others to say 'Amen' with us if we're praying together; words assembled in our minds help us to hear ourselves, and to know what we're praying when in private, even if we don't speak them out loud. But the words or other means used are only a small part of the dialogue with our all-knowing God who sees deep into our inner being. It's good to remind one another of this. Jesus told the parable about the Pharisee and the tax collector (Luke 18:10–14) to 'some who were confident of their own righteousness and looked down on everybody else' (v. 9). As well as standing as an encouragement to those whose prayers amount to a few halting words, the story is a warning to those whose confidence in their eloquent prayers is misplaced.

If you're a perfectionist, who likes to do everything 'properly, or not at all', you'll benefit from praying alongside those who have grasped the liberating truth that God is not like a stern schoolmaster waiting to respond to our prayers with 'Could do better'. You may wish to disagree, but I have a suspicion that God isn't nearly as concerned with the precise details of theological correctness in our prayers as some would like to think he is! Aware of my own perfectionist tendencies, I've found it liberating to move away from thinking about prayer as 'an activity I do' to the idea of 'prayer as relationship'. With an activity I'm either doing it or I'm not. If I see prayer as relationship, and aim to keep my heart facing in a Godward direction, that brings a different perspective. And of course 'prayer as relationship' necessarily involves listening as well as speaking.

Practising the presence of God

In the context of spiritual direction, I've come across those who appear to spend more time worrying about the inadequacy of their prayer life than they do in prayer! A reminder of the relationship aspect of prayer can bring much-needed encouragement. While I do recommend the setting aside of time for regular, focused Bible reading and prayer, my advice is to concentrate on calling to mind the reality of God's presence moment by moment (practising the presence of God), talking to him as one would to an ever-present companion. This reduces the risk of a gulf developing and, if appropriate, allows immediate expression of our frustration with our prayer life to God.

We can help one another by modelling the habit of 'prayer now' rather than 'prayer when we've got more time'. A couple of minutes —even twenty seconds—of prayer together at the time of a problem being shared reminds everyone of God's eye on those involved. 'Prayer now' is great for families. Family prayers at a meal-time are less common these days, at least in part due to changing patterns in family meals. But there's no law saying that family prayers have to be associated with food—or with that other battle-zone, bed-time! In our family, meal-time prayers were never a great success; the norm became a few words of thanks for the food. However, I used to give my sons a prayerful hug as they set out for school each day—a few seconds of committing the day to the Lord, with a brief mention of any exam or other hurdle to be surmounted. This habit survived the turbulences of adolescence and was, I believe, a source of much blessing. Although both are now grown up, they still welcome a parting hug and a prayer on leaving after a visit home.

'Prayer now' can become an integral part of the day—in the home, garage, school, supermarket, job centre, office, factory, call centre, hospital... God doesn't say 'Goodbye' at the door—he's there ahead of us, and has begun his day's activities before we've even arrived. In some workplaces, Christians are able to meet briefly for prayer and mutual support, but that's not the only way to encourage one another in workplace prayer. A look across the canteen that says 'I'm praying for you' may be just what's needed on a difficult day, and may stimulate a Christian workmate to respond by interceding for us when we're up against it with deadlines or whatever. In addition, if we're in the habit of calling to mind God's presence with us, wherever we are, it will make us more aware of what's going on spiritually, and how the Lord wants us to play our part.

I believe passionately that we need to encourage one another to know God in the present moment rather than shelving our spirituality, hoping it'll be easier when we get home, or next week, or when the children have grown up, or when we've retired... The here-and-now is where we must learn to know God's presence and experience his love, as we daily face reality and choose to honour him by the way we live.

'Where is God when I hurt?'

Encouraging and comforting one another will include modelling God's faithfulness to those for whom pain, distress or depression is obscuring the presence of 'the God of all comfort' (2 Corinthians 1:3). At times, life may feel so out of control that a person fears for their own survival or their sanity, although not everyone will be able to put this fear into words. Continuing loving acceptance, treating that person as a friend, not as a 'case'; walking alongside and sharing in ordinary activities, not homing in automatically on the problems; not being afraid to enjoy ordinary conversation, will complement any problem-orientated assistance being received from other quarters. Pain hurts. Upheaval disorientates. Intense pressure feels like a crushing weight. These are signs not of failure but of being human. Sometimes we simply need to affirm one another's sanity and continuing survival when it all feels too much.

If we've made a habit of practising the presence of God, and dealing quickly with any sin that comes to our attention, the awareness of his being alongside and hearing the cries of our hearts may be greater. But inattention and sin are not the only causes of God feeling far away. Other causes include past or recent trauma, bereavement, exhaustion, and physical or mental illness.

For some dear folk, the pain that this sense of distance produces is compounded by a burden of guilt: 'If I were really a good Christian,

I wouldn't be feeling like this.' There's a difference between knowing that God is with us and feeling that God is with us. We may be able to know that God is with us by calling to mind scriptures which assure us that he will never leave us, and that he is faithful, even when our feelings are giving a different message. Feelings matter, and it's good to acknowledge them: burying them solves nothing. But as a gold standard for truth, they're worse than useless! When answering the question 'Is God with me in this trouble?' let's encourage one another to base the answer on scripture and on God's character, not just on how we feel.

Accompanying

The book of Ruth is a story of accompanying, albeit in unusual and extreme circumstances. After the death of her husband and sons, Naomi was honest about her feelings that God had let her down (Ruth 1:20–21). Her daughter-in-law, Ruth, can't have found her great company on their long journey to Naomi's homeland. Even there, where she was a foreigner and knew no one, Ruth didn't allow herself to become absorbed with Naomi's bitterness. She set out to find enough grain for them to survive, and in the process found a husband. After Ruth had borne a son, the women of the community commented on Ruth's love for Naomi, saying that Ruth was better than seven sons (Ruth 4:15). (Study Session 5, page 181, looks at a story of a much briefer 'accompanying', and its transforming effect on the lives of the disciples whom Jesus met on the road to Emmaus.)

I can't recall who first spoke of feeling the need for 'God with skin on', but many since have used that phrase to express what it means to have brothers and sisters in Christ alongside at a difficult time. On the darkest of days, when we neither feel nor know that God is with us, the surrounding members of the body of Christ can hold us up, persisting in prayer when we've ceased to know where to begin or have lost the strength or inclination to do so. At such times the faith and love of others, sensitively communicated, are worth their weight in gold. Remember that it's possible to communicate faith and love in non-religious ways, such as offering to join a dog-walking expedition, or turning up with a cake for tea—and by 'just listening'.

We may feel obliged to sort everything out, or at least to explain it, for the sake of our own sanity as much as for anyone else's. We must resist the temptation to pursue tidy, religious answers in messy situations. Faced with a disaster or crisis, or with longer-term suffering, we ask God 'Why?'—naively assuming that if he told us exactly why we'd be able to comprehend his answer. (Try reading what God said to Job about this.) We'll slip more easily into an accompanying role if we recognize the value of simply being there—not solving, not making it better, not even having to know what it all means—just being there.

Even offering to pray can be a self-defensive way of curtailing an outpouring of intense grief or woe. We must be sensitive. 'Prayer now' may be offered wordlessly or silently while the listening is going on, as well as at the end of the conversation or on the way home. God sees our tears; spoken prayer may be superfluous—even intrusive.

We accept that Jesus was fully human as well as divine. But sometimes we're less accepting of our own humanity and that of other church members! This is especially true of leaders and others who are seen as professional walk-alongsiders. They will benefit from encouragement, not only when their own lives are painful but more generally. Pastoral crises are draining—and they rarely come one at a time. While some in the body of Christ are using their gifts and skills to help those who are suffering, others can use their resources to support, encourage and affirm the helpers. On numerous occasions the prayerful and sometimes practical backing of my support group has enabled me to go on giving out to those in acute need. This is how the body of Christ is meant to work.

Shalom

In the Old Testament, the Hebrew word *shalom* is translated 'peace', but this fails to do justice to its depth of meaning. *Shalom* includes not only health and well-being, but also harmony within oneself and in relationships. When the Greek word *eirene*, also translated 'peace', was used in the New Testament, it had this Hebrew word as its backdrop. We must allow for this when considering its meaning.

'Let the peace of Christ rule in your hearts, since as members of one body you were called to peace' (Colossians 3:15). Many men and women are unable to be at peace with others because they're not at peace with themselves. It's tempting to give such folk a wide berth, because of the disharmony they leave in their wake. But there's a place in the body of Christ for them too, even if as yet they're not ready to settle to it. We need to welcome them as best we're able, praying for them and encouraging them. If we focus all our attention on the friction they cause, and pour our energy into trying to get them under control, we risk forgetting to give them what they really need—help in finding peace with God, the foundation for *shalom* with ourselves and others.

We must urge one another to pursue the fullness of *shalom*, not merely the suspension of hostilities and smiling through gritted teeth that is sometimes labelled 'peace' in our culture. But pursuing peace isn't the same as setting out to avoid trouble. When 'Christ-in-me' collides with the evil in the world, I'm going to feel the shock waves. This is an inevitable consequence of my relationship with him. Adversity isn't automatically a sign that I'm doing something wrong, neither does it have to lead to a loss of peace. The great mystery to which saints down the ages have testified is that with Christ (I in him, and him in me) it's still possible to know *shalom* deep within while surrounded by tempestuous circumstances.

So, when we encourage one another to pursue peace, we must be sure not to confuse it with the easy life! Paul assures the Philippians that if they bring their anxieties and concerns to their heavenly Father, his peace—'the peace of God, which transcends all understanding'— will guard their hearts and minds (Philippians 4:6–7). At the time of writing, Paul was physically in prison, but his soul was garrisoned by *shalom*. That's the peace we can encourage one another to pursue.

Focus Point

- What's the difference between biblical encouragement and the world's counterfeit: flattery? Which comes most naturally to me?
- Who has spurred me on and encouraged me? You could pause to thank God for them.
- 'Let us consider how we may spur one another on towards love and good deeds. Let us not give up meeting together, as some are in the habit of doing, but let us encourage one another—and all the more as you see the Day approaching' (Hebrews 10:24–25). Over the next few weeks, you could ask the Lord to draw your attention to opportunities for encouraging others and spurring them on.
- The apostle Paul seems to have expected to receive encouragement from those he visited. Read Romans 1:12, putting yourself in the place of a member of the church in Rome as you do so. If your reaction is, 'How could I possibly encourage a great leader like him?' pray that the Lord will show you 'surprising' people nearer home who could do with some encouragement. Then ask him to show you what you could offer.
- Do you find prayer a delight or a struggle...? If you're needing encouragement in prayer, why not talk to God about it? Now! Consider adding 'prayer now' to your existing ways of praying. Is there someone you know who might be encouraged by sharing in this experiment with you?

Further reading

Joyce Huggett, *Learning the Language of Prayer*, BRF, 1994.

Rob Warner, *Walking with God: Discovering a Deeper Spirituality in Prayer*, Hodder and Stoughton, 1998.

Ruth Fowke, *Personality and Prayer*, Eagle, 1997.

1 Thessalonians 4 and 5.

6

Building Up

Therefore encourage one another and build each other up,
just as in fact you are doing.
1 THESSALONIANS 5:11

Build yourselves up in your most holy faith
and pray in the Holy Spirit.
JUDE 20

The verse above from 1 Thessalonians makes it clear that the subject of this chapter naturally follows on from the previous one. Mutual encouragement will lead to brothers and sisters in Christ being built up and, if the parts of the body of Christ are edified, the whole body is strengthened. As we'll see, it's not a matter of either individual or corporate edification needing to take priority: the two are inextricably linked, and both are tremendously important.

Many members of the body of Christ are unaware that their God-given responsibilities include edifying both themselves and others. Even in churches progressing towards every-member ministry, some may still see the responsibility for building up individuals and the body as a whole as lying with the minister. Paul recognized that he had authority from God to be used to build up (for example, 2 Corinthians 13:10), but he never implied that he, or leaders in general, should be doing all the building. Leaders are gifted by God in diverse ways in order that they may 'prepare God's people for works of service [*diakonia*, ministry] so that the body of Christ may be built up' (Ephesians 4:12). The equipping of church leaders is intended to lead to the equipping of *all* members for 'body-building ministry', not just to more or better leader-ministry.

Aim to build

Building is one of the apostle Paul's recurring themes, especially in his letters to the Corinthian and Ephesian churches. The Greek word he uses figuratively when writing about building up is the same word used for building a house. Translators have tried to capture its meaning in a variety of ways according to the context, and have written about edifying, strengthening and emboldening one another and the Church.

What comes over is *a sense of intention*. It's a focused approach: do things that you know help to build people up; make building a clear aim and do it actively and intentionally. For example, in Romans 14:19 Paul's plea is to 'make every effort to do what leads to peace and to mutual edification', and he continues, 'We who are strong ought to bear with the failings of the weak and not to please ourselves. Each of us should please his neighbour for his good, to build him up' (Romans 15:1–2). The context is of a disagreement about whether or not Jewish food laws had to be observed by Christians. Feelings were running high, and both sides of the heated debate felt that 'right'—and no doubt God, too!—was on their side. Paul's response was to question the attitudes of those involved, and to suggest that there were higher priorities than being in the right. The possible lessons from a different but equally difficult dilemma over food are explored in Study Session 6 (page 183).

What is the Father doing?

The late John Wimber highlighted Jesus' words about doing what he saw the Father doing (John 5:19). In seeking to play our part in building, it's vital that we don't neglect to ask God what *his* plans are. He may show us something of the bigger picture; he may require us to be patient and faithful, having shown us no more than where to lay the next 'brick'. But if we're open to his leading, our building will have eternal significance.

The whole body builds itself up 'as each part does its work' (Ephesians 4:16), but the work of building does need to be under the direction of the Master Builder who also empowers the growth. Paul saw himself and Apollos as 'God's fellow workers', collaborating with God in his building, but being careful to use only the foundations that God had already laid in Jesus Christ (1 Corinthians 3:6–11). In the same way, the initiative and creativity God gives us today are best used with an eye to where and how God is at work, and the direction and pace he is setting.

Resources for building

Agape-love is clearly indispensable at every stage, but what else is there?

God's word builds up

Saying farewell to the Ephesian elders, Paul said: 'Now I commit you to God and to the word of his grace, which can build you up and give you an inheritance among all those who are sanctified' (Acts 20:32). In his letter, he exhorted them to 'be filled with the Spirit', and went on to urge them to 'speak to one another with psalms, hymns and spiritual songs' (Ephesians 5:18–19). Paul wrote in similar vein to the Colossians: 'Let the word of Christ dwell in you richly as you teach and admonish one another with all wisdom, and as you sing psalms, hymns and spiritual songs with gratitude in your hearts to God' (Colossians 3:16). God's word has a key role in building up.

Singing scripture-based hymns and songs is a great way to allow the word of Christ to dwell richly. I expect you find, as I do, that it's not unusual for words sung in church on Sunday to keep coming back during the week. Some of the psalms I sang in the church choir as a teenager have formed an indelible imprint on my memory, and I'm grateful for that.

Individual and shared Bible study will play an important part in being built up. It's good to read the scriptures devotionally, too. By this I mean reading with the heart, not just the mind, and giving God time to speak into our situation. Devotional reading flows comfortably in and out of prayer, and strengthens our relationship with God—not just our understanding about him. Are there those among your housegroup, friends or family who might welcome being introduced to this style of reading, if it's new to them?

Let's note in passing that, although Bible verses and passages will have a unique and indispensable place in our sharing of what God has to say, he doesn't just speak through the scriptures. God spoke our world into being; Jesus came as the Word incarnate; God continues to speak to individuals and churches today through the operation of his Holy Spirit. (See more on this and the comments on 'weighing and testing' with regard to prophecy, page 103.) Even words quoted directly from scripture must be scrutinized prayerfully to ensure that they are being applied correctly, and are not being used manipulatively or in any other way contrary to God's purposes. (See how Satan misused scripture when he tempted Jesus, Matthew 4:6.)

Teaching

Many folk, on hearing the word 'teaching', immediately think in terms of preaching and other formal instruction. Worthwhile as these are, they're only a part of the spectrum. Of course, teaching amounts to much more than words but, even in terms of spoken teaching, the proportion given by leaders gifted and appointed for such work is intended to be only a fraction of the ongoing teaching within the body of Christ.

Paul didn't want the members of the new churches sitting around, growing in frustration, waiting for the expert to turn up and teach them—he wanted to galvanize them all into action! Sadly, in some parts of the Church, much energy is expended in restraining rather than letting loose the people of God. The concerns expressed by

Roland Allen in the early 20th century about world mission methods are sadly still of relevance to today's Church: 'We dread the possible mistakes of individual zeal. The result is that our converts hesitate to speak of religion to others. They throw the responsibility upon the licensed evangelist and "the mission"' (Roland Allen, *Missionary Methods: St Paul's or Ours?* World Dominion Press, 1912). Good teachers, like good parents, aim to impart competence so that they are no longer needed. Teaching that succeeds only in impressing others with the teacher's knowledge or expertise is of little long-term value and may actually be disabling.

Kathy Galloway, formerly warden of Iona Abbey and a member of the Iona Community, has pointed out that for many the church is 'the only part of their lives where they are treated as children' (Revd Kathy Galloway in *Communities of Hope*, edited by Russell Bowman-Eadie and Graham Dodds). She stresses the importance of encouraging men and women to grow up in their faith, rather than infantilizing them. She also draws attention to the many occasions on which Jesus asked a question rather than giving an answer.

Mutual edification

Wise teachers down the ages have sought to stimulate the development of their pupils' own reasoning and decision-making capacities by means of thought-provoking questions. As sisters and brothers in Christ, we can explore questions together—such as 'What is God like?'—searching the scriptures, teasing out answers as part of our journey of exploration. And in all this we can reassure one another that God has undertaken to give wisdom to those who ask for it (James 1:5).

Within our church prayer ministry team, we invite those who have learned something, whether by attending a course or through personal experience, to share it with the rest of us. Sometimes the topic has already been covered in the team's teaching sessions, but a truth shared by someone for whom it has recently come alive is much more memorable than the same truth taught as part of a programme. As a bonus, the person who shares and builds others up is usually also encouraged and built up in the process. The same dynamic applies in home groups, or other group settings which offer opportunities for sharing.

Mutual edification works most effectively within a framework of accountability. Over the years, I've been present in a number of groups in which the sharing of a mixture of homespun theories, garbled pseudo-science and misremembered scriptures has been anything but edifying! I'm not advocating the sort of tight control that allows only 'perfect' contributions—members need opportunities to think out loud and to clarify their understanding without getting jumped on. But we have a responsibility not only to teach truth but also to train others to discover truth for themselves. In addition, those who are in a muddle will benefit from some gentle redirection.

Admonishing

The Greek verb *noutheteo* means 'to put in mind, warn or admonish'. Admonition (*nouthesia*) was seen by Paul as a necessary part of winning back errant members of the church (see, for example, 1 Thessalonians 5:14). James was expressing a similar idea when he wrote about bringing back those who had wandered from the truth (James 5:19–20). Paul told Titus to warn anyone who was being divisive (Titus 3:10). When he said that fathers should bring up their children 'in the training and instruction of the Lord' (Ephesians 6:4), he was using the same word, there translated 'instruction'. (See also Acts 20:31 and Colossians 1:28.)

Paul sees directing one another towards truth as a normal activity, not just for leaders but for all within the body of Christ: 'I myself am convinced, my brothers, that you yourselves are full of goodness, complete in knowledge and competent to instruct [KJV: admonish] one another' (Romans 15:14); 'Let the word of Christ dwell in you richly as you teach and admonish one another with all wisdom' (Colossians 3:16). We may teach and admonish only on the basis that the word of Christ *is* dwelling in us richly, bringing his wisdom. If we work on any other basis, such as that our opinions are better or more important than those of others, we'll be building dangerous foundations.

Everyday relationships

We're inclined to read stories such as the one about Philip being miraculously on hand when the Ethiopian eunuch wanted someone to help him understand the scriptures (Acts 8:26–35) and think 'I could never do that!' This attitude not only closes the door on God using us in equally surprising ways, but may also lead us to undervalue the effect of the contacts we have day by day. Much edifying can happen informally within ordinary relationships, and in most it's likely to be our manner of life, not just our words, that makes the impact. Living the gospel is much more powerful than proclamation alone.

If we're allowing God's word to influence our thinking and our behaviour, we won't find it odd to refer to this in conversation. The Old Testament people of God were instructed to fix his words in their hearts and minds, and to make them part of their daily conversation, both in the home and when out and about (Deuteronomy 11:18–19). Paul urged the Colossians, 'Let your conversation be always full of grace, seasoned with salt' (Colossians 4:6). To the Ephesians he wrote, 'Do not let any unwholesome talk come out of your mouths, but only what is helpful for building others up according to their needs, that it may benefit those who listen' (Ephesians 4:29). Jesus taught that one day we'll be called to account for our careless use of words (Matthew 12:36). These verses taken together set quite a standard for our conversation!

Remembering the letters from Paul to Timothy, what about the potential for encouraging one another and building one another up through letters or e-mails? It's many years since Jane was a missionary overseas, but when I asked her what she felt had built her up, she mentioned the weekly letter from a lady in her home church. And it's not just missionaries who appreciate letters! Those who are unable to meet for fellowship, or are away from home studying or working, can be encouraged and built up in this way. The fact that we're taking the trouble to stay in touch will underline the fact that we love them—that it's not a matter of 'out of sight, out of mind'.

Testimony is a powerful building tool—and not just the prepared sort of testimony given by arrangement in a church gathering. If we're sensitive to the leading of the Holy Spirit, we'll find we're sharing our testimony in conversation with our sisters and brothers in Christ for their edification, as well as informally with those who are not yet believers. Neither do I mean only the 'how I came to Christ' sort of testimony. Some years ago I went to a service in another church, and heard an octogenarian member of the congregation give his testimony. It was a lovely story about how he had become a Christian in his twenties, but it left me feeling rather sad. It gave the impression that nothing much had happened since, which I knew to be untrue. If God is at work in our lives day by day, we can bear witness to that and build up the body of Christ as we do so. And if the only testimony we're able to give relates to events months or years ago, shouldn't we be asking why?

Choosing to grow

Most of the scripture references to building up refer to building one another up, and to building up the body of Christ as a whole, but each of us also has a part to play in our own edification. This is brought home by Jude, writing to some Christians who were in danger of being seduced by a gospel that did not include personal holiness: 'Dear friends, carefully build yourselves up in this most holy faith by praying in the Holy Spirit, staying right at the centre of God's love, keeping your arms open and outstretched, ready for the mercy of our Master, Jesus Christ' (Jude 20–21, THE MESSAGE).

Personal responsibility

It is our responsibility to choose to stay in the centre of God's love rather than 'testing the boundaries', as wilful children are wont to do.

Not surprisingly, those who are doing all they can to be built up in their faith will be much more responsive to encouragement and edification offered by others. In contrast, those who prefer being wilful children don't tend to welcome assistance with growing up, although they may whine enviously about those whom they see enjoying the benefits of a mature faith.

The writer to the Hebrews takes up the theme of personal responsibility for moving on. He reprimands his readers for sitting around like babies waiting to be fed when they should be grown up and able to teach others. Their spiritual 'muscles' are flabby instead of well-developed by regular use (Hebrews 5:11–14). Paul, writing to Timothy, tells him straight, 'Train yourself to be godly' (1 Timothy 4:7). He goes on (v. 8) to explain that 'physical training is of some value, but godliness has value for all things, holding promise for both the present life and the life to come'.

In his second letter, Paul reminds Timothy of the responsibility to 'fan into flame' the gift he has received, before teaching him that God has given all his children 'a spirit of power, of love and of self-discipline' (2 Timothy 1:7). Centuries before, Solomon had observed, 'Like a city whose walls are broken down is a man who lacks self-control' (Proverbs 25:28). The resources are available, the opportunities are there. It's up to us to choose to 'go for it'—and to encourage one another in fighting the spiritual flab!

The iceberg principle

When Christians are enthusiastic about serving and ministering, and others are keen for them to use their gifts to the fullest possible extent, much good can be done. But serving and ministering mustn't happen at the expense of being built up. It's true that building up may happen as a consequence of serving, but if the serving degenerates into an exhausting treadmill which drains spiritually, physically and emotionally, and never leaves any time for 'refilling', there will be trouble ahead.

For an iceberg, it's the 90 per cent hidden below the water-line that provides stability for the visible ten per cent. In the same way, it's the less visible aspects of our life that provide the essential under-girding for our serving and public activities—the daily personal and spiritual disciplines; the regular receiving from God by his Holy Spirit and through the ministry of others; time set aside for food, rest, play and recreation. As part of choosing to grow, it's good to check out from time to time with God (maybe with the help of a friend) whether or not our lifestyle has the ingredients necessary for stability. If not, we're heading for a crisis—and sooner rather than later.

In some parts of the world, even Christian leaders have only parts of the Bible available, and there are few if any Christian books in local languages. Those of us who are spoiled for choice have no excuse. I know that some folk are less enthusiastic about books, and prefer listening to speakers at meetings or at home on tape or video. Others find participating in workshops and group events much more bene-ficial. The key question is not whether we're doing the same as the next person, but whether we're making what use we can of the resources at our disposal.

Selecting our role models

Another aspect of the choice to grow and be built up is a willingness to review what may have been an unconscious selection of role models. Take a moment to think: is there someone on whom you've modelled your style, your behaviour, your expression of spirituality? These days, mentoring is in vogue in the secular world, and in some churches and organizations inexperienced leaders are able to spend time with more expert leaders. This may be of value—depending on what's being learned. But even if there is no formal mentoring arrangement, young leaders and other young Christians will have been modelling themselves to a greater or lesser extent, consciously or unconsciously, on those whom they admire.

If we've modelled ourselves on certain individuals or groups, it would be good to reflect on why we've selected them. Is it because they are Christ-like? Or have we been attracted to them because they are popular, or appear to have the ear of influential people? If our responsibilities include discipling or mentoring others, we'll need to check that we're pointing them to Christ, not attracting followers of our own. Ultimately, all such relationships have to be judged by their fruit. Paul knew that he was an imperfect example, but he was bold enough to say, 'Follow my example'—with the rider, 'as I follow the example of Christ' (1 Corinthians 11:1; see also 2 Thessalonians 3:7–9; Hebrews 13:7).

Timothy had been mentored by Paul, spending time with him, learning from his example, being pointed to Christ. Paul now felt confident that Timothy would be able to do the same for others (see 1 Corinthians 4:14–17). The process had been similar for the Thessalonian Christians, whom Paul saw as 'a model to all the believers in Macedonia and Achaia' (1 Thessalonians 1:6–7). In New Testament times, there was a much greater emphasis on teaching by example. Then it was a necessity, because of the limited availability of alternatives. Today, although the practice of mentoring is growing, this rarely includes the intensity of contact experienced by Paul and Timothy. Is this purely because of the profusion of alternatives, or might a reluctance on the part of leaders to open their lives to close scrutiny also be a factor?

Living on a building site

In preparation for writing this chapter, I asked some friends to reflect on how they had been built up. Most in some way underlined the value of close relationships with other Christians. One person specifically mentioned that friends sometimes helped her with 'the knocking down of those bits which shouldn't be encouraged to grow'! Some commented that it was beneficial when others acknowledged the building up that had been taking place that they hadn't themselves noticed.

Another theme in the answers was that people had been built up by being offered opportunities to exercise their spiritual gifts. This will have been doubly worthwhile, having enabled them also to contribute to building up the body of Christ; spiritual gifts are, after all, given for the common good (1 Corinthians 12:7). Paul wrote to the Ephesians that Christ had gifted some to be apostles, prophets, evangelists, pastors and teachers 'to prepare God's people for works of service [*diakonia*], so that the body of Christ may be built up' (Ephesians 4:11–12).

'Try to excel in gifts that build up the church,' Paul urged the Corinthians (1 Corinthians 14:12). In particular, he urged them to use the gift of prophecy, seeing it as a means of strengthening, encouraging, comforting and edifying the church (1 Corinthians 14:3–5). Nowadays, some see prophecy as a source of *dis*comfort and undermining. Concerns are usually related, often justifiably, to the infallible 'thus saith the Lord' approach. This style is common in the Old Testament: one individual proclaimed God's word authoritatively —sometimes a lone voice speaking to a whole nation. In the New Testament, however, Paul emphasized the need for weighing and testing (1 Corinthians 14:29; 1 Thessalonians 5:19–21), presumably to distinguish God-given prophecies from similar-sounding insights or words. The implication is that we can expect at least some of what we hear from God to be less clear-cut.

Spirit-led discernment is necessary, lest anxiety lead to rejecting everything or gullibility lead to unquestioning acceptance. This is particularly true today, when much that comes under the umbrella heading of prophecy could be described as 'subjective' rather than 'authoritative'. A member of the body of Christ may say, 'I sense that God is saying...', or, 'As I was praying, I had a picture of...', or, 'I feel that God might be wanting us to focus on such-and-such'. Paul's instruction is that 'the others should weigh carefully what is said' (1 Corinthians 14:29). The weighing is to be done prayerfully by the body of Christ, led by the leaders. It isn't always easy; life on a building site can't always be 'tidy'.

Let's thank God that we have the Bible as our abiding reference point. Jesus, 'the good shepherd', spoke of his sheep knowing and listening to his voice (John 10:3, 4, 16, 27. For additional insights, see Galatians 1:8; 1 Timothy 4:1–3; 1 John 4:1–3). Familiarity with

God's voice speaking through scripture will help us to recognize it when he speaks in other ways. God's nature does not change; he will not say things that are 'out of character'. Neither is he perverse: if we ask him for clarification he will answer, although not necessarily according to the timescale we had in mind. Speaking about false prophets, Jesus said that they would be known by their fruit (Matthew 7:15–20). In our age of instant everything, we'd really prefer to know straight away whether or not something is the real thing. The idea of waiting to see what fruit comes sounds a bit slow!

Jesus our model

When all is said and done, our model for building up must be Jesus. He persevered in building up his disciples, right to the end—even though they had made mistakes, demonstrated ungodly attitudes and shown unenlightened self-interest.

The relationships Jesus built with those who followed him were foundational to their learning. 'Walk with me and work with me,' he said, 'watch how I do it... Keep company with me and you'll learn to live freely and lightly' (Matthew 11:29–30, THE MESSAGE). The challenging questions he asked them, the pictures he used (for example, John 10:11—'I am the good shepherd'; also the other 'I ams' of John's Gospel), the way he extended their thinking (for example, 'You give them something to eat', Mark 6:37), his sending them off in pairs to gain experience of preaching and healing—all this will have contributed to their edification. It's striking that so little of what they are recorded as having gained from Jesus seems to have been in the form of sermon-style teaching!

Jesus built up those who let him down

Jesus knew that the disciples would desert him or deny him when the heat was on. But *still* he built them up. This is particularly obvious during the time they spent together in the upper room (John 13—17).

Luke records a detail from these hours that John omits. Prior to Peter's protestation that he would go with Jesus to prison and death, Jesus had said to Peter, 'Simon, Simon, Satan has asked to sift you [plural] as wheat. But I have prayed for you, Simon, that your faith may not fail. And when you [singular] have turned back, strengthen your brothers' (Luke 22:31–32). Jesus was building Peter up by revealing the work he had for him to do and the trust he was placing in him as a future leader. When Peter met his resurrected Lord on the seashore, Jesus continued to build him up in the same way: 'Feed my lambs... Take care of my sheep... Feed my sheep' (John 21:15–17). He knew that Peter, though he had denied Jesus, had the capacity to strengthen (establish) the others who were to share in the leadership of the early Church.

Is it possible that many of those whom we currently find less than helpful, or even prone to deserting us at crucial moments, would be better able to serve God and bless the body of Christ if they were to be consistently built up and encouraged to fulfil their potential in the way Peter was by Jesus? Do we need to rethink our approach to building one another up—not just directing our efforts towards those who are already being helpful, getting it right (whatever 'it' is) and proving fruitful, but building up those who have as yet shown no potential, and whose unreliability is as legendary as Peter's?

Jesus continues to offer the invitation to keep company with him, to walk and work with him, watching how he does it. He lovingly edifies those of us who let him down time after time. Are we willing to do likewise?

Focus Point

- Is my serving and ministering adequately resourced by the less visible aspects of my life? See 'The iceberg principle', page 100.
- What are the gifts that God has given me for the edification of the Church? Take time over answering this question. Pray it through. Ask your housegroup or other friends to pray it through, too. Perhaps you could set time aside at a series of meetings to help discern one another's gifts, and make it a habit to encourage group members to exercise their gifts for everyone's benefit. (1 Corinthians 12—14 would be a worthwhile place to start.)
- Think back to 'hospitality, teaching and midwifery' (Chapter 2, page 38). Reflect on their meaning, and what you have to offer to others which could encourage them and build them up.
- Reflect on the part played by Timothy's grandmother Lois, his mother Eunice and others (2 Timothy 1:5; 3:14–17) and also by Priscilla and Aquila in explaining things to Apollos, who then went on to build up many others (Acts 18:24–28).
- Paul wrote to the church at Corinth: 'Follow my example, as I follow the example of Christ' (1 Corinthians 11:1). If someone spent a lot of time with me and learned to behave as I do, what would they be learning, and would I want them to teach it to others?

Further reading

Kathy Dice, *Personal Devotion: Taking God's Word to Heart*, from the Bible 101 series for small groups, Willow Creek Association, IVP, 2000.

Eugene H. Peterson, *The Wisdom of Each Other: A Conversation Between Spiritual Friends*, Zondervan, 1998.

As an introduction to many edifying writers from across the centuries, try the book edited by Richard Foster and James Bryan Smith, *Devotional Classics: Selected Readings for Individuals and Groups*, Hodder and Stoughton, 1993.

2 Timothy.

7

Moving On Together

> Therefore... let us throw off everything that hinders and the sin
> that so easily entangles, and let us run with perseverance the
> race marked out for us. Let us fix our eyes on Jesus.
>
> HEBREWS 12:1–2

The verses above come after the writer to the Hebrews' great gallery of
faith (Hebrews 11). In relatively few words he has sketched out
numerous personal stories of faith-in-action, usually in difficult or
apparently impossible circumstances. 'Therefore,' he continues, 'since
we are surrounded by such a great cloud of witnesses, let us throw off
everything that hinders…'

Everything that hinders

Maybe these verses from Hebrews are very familiar—you know their
context well, and have heard many sermons exhorting you to fix your
eyes on Jesus, 'the author and perfecter of our faith' (Hebrews 12:2).
If so, that's great! But it would be good to pause for a moment and
ask yourself if you've ever allowed the full implications of the first
verse to soak deep into your soul. It's one of the most challenging
calls to discipleship in the Bible: 'Let us throw off everything that
hinders and the sin that so easily entangles, and let us run with
perseverance the race marked out for us.'

Running the race marked out

These words challenge us to ask ourselves how much we really want to grow in grace and maturity. Do we want it enough to throw off everything—yes, *everything*—that hinders? Do we turn away from sin as soon as we see it coming, or do we sometimes entertain it long enough to risk becoming entangled? Are we committed to running with perseverance the race marked out for us, or do we have at least one eye looking out for an easier route, avoiding rough terrain?

Some people hold that moderation is a key principle. They see a commitment to wholehearted pressing on in pursuit of any cause as inherently unbalanced, and mutter about the dangers of fanaticism. This reveals a serious misunderstanding. God is good; our heavenly Father is to be trusted. He knows us through and through—he made us, he has gifted and equipped us. He knows us better than we know ourselves. He knows our capabilities and where we're vulnerable. He knows that we need different nourishing and equipping at different stages. His plans for us are good, and include not only challenges but also times of refreshment and rest. Wholehearted commitment to following the way he has marked out for us will be beneficial, not destructive. The way may at times be hard; if it involves opposition and persecution, blood may be shed, and some of it may be ours. But if we persevere in following God's leading, empowered by the Holy Spirit, we'll be able to see it through.

Paul wasn't afraid of being seen as unbalanced on account of his single-minded devotion to Christ. 'You've all been to the stadium and seen the athletes race,' he wrote to the Christians at Corinth. 'Everyone runs; one wins. Run to win. All good athletes train hard. They do it for a gold medal that tarnishes and fades. You're after one that's gold eternally.' Warming to his theme, Paul continued: 'I don't know about you, but I'm running hard for the finish line. I'm giving it everything I've got. No sloppy living for me! I'm staying alert and in top condition. I'm not going to be caught napping, telling everyone else all about it and then missing out myself' (1 Corinthians 9:24–27, THE MESSAGE).

Throwing off everything that hinders, turning away from sin and seeking to follow Christ wholeheartedly... all these things honour God and serve his purposes. By contrast, drivenness (which may be due to emotional pain, or a desire to shore up a fragile self-worth with achievement) may take us along perilous tracks outside God's plan. If we're driven, we may do right but in the wrong way or at a damaging pace. Drivenness may even lead to the sort of fanaticism that gives religion a bad name. It does not honour God or serve his purposes. Drivenness flows out of our fallen nature, our pain and our neediness, and is a counterfeit of the wholehearted pressing on to which we're called as disciples of Christ.

Facing hardship

'Endure hardship as discipline,' continues the writer to the Hebrews (12:7), stressing that this is part of God's fatherly care for us. It's important to note that he is writing about discipline, not punishment. Sometimes these words are wrongly used as if they were interchangeable. Punishment is received as a consequence of wrongdoing, whereas discipline is part of the training required to develop the sort of character needed to resist temptation and to pursue good. It's also important to note that the race is for those who are already saved; it's not a race towards getting saved one day. To put it in theological terms, participation in the race will contribute to our sanctification (holy-making), but we have to accept our justification (by faith, possible only because Christ shed his blood for us, Romans 5:1, 9) before we begin.

If we're to run the race God has marked out for us, we must be willing to choose to do right whatever the hardships involved; to embrace, not just tolerate, change; to work from a position of trust, even when circumstances appear to raise questions about God's character. I'm sure I'm not alone in finding this difficult at times. I've found it helpful to keep a journal, noting dilemmas, difficulties and questions that come up, as well as answers to prayer and the alleluias. The journal helps me not to lose sight of unresolved issues, and this means I'm more likely to notice answers when they come along.

The reality of our Christian 'race' is that some of it is bound to be uphill. It may take us through what looks like impenetrable jungle. We risk losing our way, or being injured and temporarily unable to continue. Faced with this, some settle for less than wholehearted discipleship, finding it too difficult to sustain alone.

The good news is that Jesus, the 'pioneer' of our faith (Hebrews 12:2, RSV), is leading the way and has promised to be with us. What's more, the Bible repeatedly draws attention to the corporate dimension of spiritual life which is part of God's plan and intention for his people. *I don't have to face the struggles and conflicts alone.* Meeting together along the way and urging one another on are meant to be a normal part of the Christian 'race' or 'journey'. The writer to the Hebrews warns his readers not to give up meeting together, and continues, 'Let us encourage one another—and all the more as you see the Day approaching' (Hebrews 10:25).

Selecting a training partner

Fifty years ago it was very unusual to see anyone out jogging, and marathon races were relatively unusual. Nowadays, opportunities for competitive long-distance running abound, and there are annual marathon races in cities the world over. Many organizers also put on a 'fun run' for those who prefer a less arduous training pattern, or who want to dress up in strange costumes. The fun runners have a great time, and often raise lots of money for good causes, but the spectators and participants know that when compared with national or Olympic glory, a fun run doesn't even come close.

The Christian life has plenty of fun moments, but our approach to training needs to be closer to that of a dedicated marathon runner than to that of a fun runner. Serious athletes take care in selecting their training partners, looking out for those who are committed to the necessary hard work—week in, week out—and who are prepared to accept certain lifestyle limitations. Time out for fun and relaxation has a place, but they take care that it doesn't affect their race performance. They really are committed to throwing off everything that hinders. They have a clear focus: the race takes priority.

Paul wrote to the Philippians: 'Stick with me, friends. Keep track of those you see running this same course, headed for this same goal' (Philippians 3:17, THE MESSAGE). What about us? Are we on the spiritual equivalent of a fun run—having a good time jogging along, masquerading as a chicken or Mickey Mouse, supporting a good cause? Or is it the race marked out for us by God, not just doing worthy things but serving his purposes, in the company of athletes who are committed to keeping 'in step with the Spirit' (Galatians 5:25)?

Faced with this sort of question, some feel led to seek out a spiritual director to help them as they try to discern and respond to God's call. This isn't a move I'd wish to discourage, but it's my passion to see the body of Christ working together in such a way that it's normal for many of the issues that are brought to spiritual directors to be addressed within the context of 'ordinary' fellowship.

A spiritual director offers a degree of detachment, which is valuable and may even be advisable. For example, I act as spiritual director to a small number of church leaders who find it worthwhile to have a 'safe pair of ears' outside their own congregation. A spiritual director is like a coach who offers help with fitness and technique in the pauses between races. By contrast, training partners are slogging round the same circuit; they see each other when out of sight of the coach. In the same way, those who occasionally see us on a Saturday night or a Monday morning—not just in our more focused moments —may have unique insights concerning our spiritual state and be able to offer encouragement or criticism along the way, just when it's needed.

'Training partners' are beneficial in other ways, too. For example, although it's a joy to go to a stimulating or uplifting conference, or to make a retreat and come home brimming over with blessing, we're then faced with the task of integrating all that we've learned or received from God with our everyday lives. Sharing it with others will help us to reflect on what has been gained; having them take an interest as we face the daily battle of faithfulness in applying it will be even more valuable.

Straight talking

Reading Paul's letters to Timothy, it seems that he was expecting his 'son in the faith' to be receptive of his numerous exhortations. Paul clearly felt that their relationship was close enough for him to write boldly. Note that he even presumed to comment on Timothy's diet. 'Use a little wine because of your stomach and your frequent illnesses,' he advised (1 Timothy 5:23). By the way, Kenneth Leech in his classic book on spiritual direction, *Soul Friend* (SPCK, 1977), points out that spiritual directors down the ages have always paid attention to their directees' eating, sleeping and relaxing because of the effect these have on the health or otherwise of the spiritual life.

In his second letter, Paul drew parallels with a soldier, a champion athlete and a hard-working farmer looking forward to a share of the crops (2 Timothy 2:3–6). He then went on to exhort Timothy to 'avoid godless chatter' (2:16) and to 'flee the evil desires of youth', encouraging him rather to 'pursue righteousness, faith, love and peace' (2:22). The letters of Paul the experienced apostle to Timothy the younger church leader have a lot to teach us about building one another up, and I recommend taking time to read and ponder them. You could use Study Session 7 as part of this (page 184).

I could have quoted numerous other strong exhortations; Paul didn't pull his punches. But let's notice how they're framed. There are verses expressing Paul's confidence in Timothy, his 'true son in the faith' (1 Timothy 1:2), and reminding him both of the prophecies once made about him and the gifts he has received from God (1:18, 4:14). Paul's second letter includes even more encouraging words.

Reading Paul's letters to Timothy with modern eyes, how do you feel about what he had to say? As you consider what it might have been like to be on the receiving end of these letters, does the word 'criticism' come to mind? If so, how do you feel about it? Many today would hold that the eleventh commandment should be 'Thou shalt not criticize', and having been a member of a church leadership team I know the feeling! But is there perhaps a danger of throwing the baby out with the bathwater?

Criticism—not for Christians, surely?

The oft-quoted verse about 'speaking the truth in love' (Ephesians 4:15) may or may not be advocating loving criticism (see my comments in Chapter 3). Whatever the correct interpretation, the content of Paul's letters is ample evidence that he saw honest criticism as necessary in urging fellow Christians on beyond their spiritual infancy and in challenging unhealthy attitudes within the body of Christ. Having their best interests at heart, he was prepared to write or speak hard things when that was appropriate. He gave plenty of encouragement to the first-century churches and their leaders, but he was also faithful in warning those he saw as being on a dangerous path, because he wanted them to grow, to be strong and to share with him in advancing God's Kingdom—and because he loved them.

My experience among Christians today in a variety of churches and organizations is that there is considerable reluctance to enter into constructive criticism. Criticism has fallen into disrepute through misuse and abuse, rather like sex and power. It's a regrettable fact that we're often much harder on those who share our own failings. Those of us who are parents may have been remonstrating with a child about their habit of leaving school assignments to the last minute, or some other unwelcome tendency, only to have a flashback to our own mother or father saying similar things to us.

Being criticized is rarely a comfortable experience, but if we're keen to reach a level of competence—in any field—we're likely to think that the gain is worth the pain. I was able to improve my first book considerably because sisters and brothers in Christ took me seriously when I asked for criticism. As the book moved towards publication, Naomi Starkey (one of BRF's editors) criticized constructively, sharing generously of her expertise. As I write, the same refining process is already under way for this book, and I'm tremendously grateful. 'Faithful are the wounds of a friend' (Proverbs 27:6, RSV).

When considering voicing criticism, I try to examine what I feel I need to say under three headings. First, is the substance of my criticism accurate? Second, is it important—does it matter? Third, what is in my heart as I consider giving criticism—are my motives pure? If, after sieving my intentions in this way, I feel that the criticism is both true and necessary, and being given in the right spirit, I look for an opportunity to talk things through. Sadly, some are willing to offer plenty of criticism—but only in gossiping about those to whom it refers. For others, the notion that criticism is automatically a sin is so ingrained that they are reluctant or unable to offer constructive criticism, even when specifically invited to do so.

Not judging

Some people have tried to use Jesus' words about taking the plank out of our own eye before attempting to help with a speck of sawdust in someone else's (Matthew 7:3–5; Luke 6:41–42) to forbid all criticism. Their interpretation is that we are not allowed to criticize others until we have attained perfection ourselves—which means never! However, the context gives us the key: Jesus' words follow a command not to judge (and, in Luke's Gospel, a command to forgive instead of condemning). But what's the difference between judging and criticizing?

The occasion when Jesus was presented with a woman caught in the act of adultery can help us to think this through. Surrounded by the religious leaders, Jesus said, 'If anyone of you is without sin, let him be the first to throw a stone at her.' It is recorded that the hearers began to leave, the older ones first, until Jesus was alone with the woman. 'Has no one condemned you?' he asked. 'No one, sir,' replied the woman. '"Then neither do I condemn you," Jesus declared. "Go now and leave your life of sin"' (John 8:3–11).

Jesus was straight with the woman: 'Stop sinning.' But he didn't condemn her. If we're not sure about our motives when we consider criticizing someone, we can examine our hearts using this story, asking ourselves: are we shaping up, ready to throw a stone? If so, our attitude is one of judgment and condemnation, and we must sort that out with God—urgently! We can't possibly offer loving, honest criticism which will be to our brother or sister's good with such evil in our hearts.

If what we find in our hearts is a concern for the other person's well-being, we'll need to ask the Lord to show us how to proceed—and to be willing to handle it his way. He may be asking us to pray, or to provide other support for the person concerned while he leads them through the issues over a period of time. He may (and this is for those who feel weak at the knees at the thought of voicing criticism) be asking us to take our courage in both hands and say something.

Timing matters

I have learned from experience, including not a few mistakes, that criticism is usually best delivered after some thought and not as an instantaneous response. Even when it's invited, or the context is one of general discussion about 'how it went', it's best to pause briefly to discern whether an openness to criticism really is there. 'Tell me what you think' may be sincerely meant, or it may be a nervous plea for affirmation. It should be obvious that last thing at night is not a good time to deal with weighty matters, especially when criticism is on the agenda. But how many church members choose home-time after an evening service or meeting to buttonhole leaders about ongoing concerns?

It's often said that, when criticizing, it's best to begin with positive comments, so that the person affected realizes that they're not being seen as 'all bad'. This may be so in some cases, but when positive affirming statements are accompanied by overtly nervous body language, I can hear the 'But...' coming—and wish the criticizer would get on with it!

Over the years I've received plenty of criticism, as well as encouragement, from my singing teacher. Last year, however, I suffered a prolonged bout of laryngitis. My voice was scratchy, and I was becoming concerned about the time it was taking to return to full strength. At that point, telling me that my singing was not up to the mark would have been counter-productive. A hospital check-up revealed only a minor problem and confirmed that the gentle exercise regime I was following with the teacher was the right route to recovery. As my voice gained in strength, a more critical approach to my singing became appropriate once again. In the same way, we'll want to be sensitive to the broader picture when considering a criticism. But if there always seems to be a 'good reason' why someone is unable to do as they said they would, or is operating below an agreed standard, the situation warrants gentle exploration even at the risk of being called 'insensitive'.

A sense of partnership

To be truly effective, criticism needs to be given and received within the 'elasticity' of *agape*-love. The other golden rule regarding the giving of criticism is to criticize the person's actions rather than the person themselves. 'I haven't understood your point' is less wounding than 'I can't understand you.' Beyond that, it's difficult to make many generalizations about how to criticize, because the pre-existing relationship between those concerned will be a major factor in determining the best approach.

It may be worth asking the person about to be criticized for their views before jumping in at the deep end. For example, they may be equally unhappy about the way they led a particular meeting, and leap at the chance to talk it through; they may be seeing the magazine article as an unsatisfactory 'best I can do in the time available' effort, and be only too glad to receive constructive input. Allowing the person we intend to criticize to air their own thoughts first will let them know that their views are valued by us, and may actually change our perspective on the issues. If, having heard how they're seeing things, we feel it's right to go ahead with the criticism, it will then come as part of a friendly discussion between two partners with shared concerns; it's less likely to evoke memories of being confronted by a school teacher and told, 'That's not good enough!'

If the relationship is already tense, with a history of minor skirmishes, any criticism—however constructive, well-meant, and carefully delivered—is likely to be unproductive. Is there another team member with a better relationship who is in a position to take things forward—if the issues are significant enough to warrant that? Whether or not that is so, it will be important to work on the relationship in so far as that is possible, in order that the body of Christ is not scarred by it—not just so that you'll be in a better position to criticize the person in future!

Those who can't cope with criticism

Those who are wanting to 'throw off everything that hinders' in order to move on will welcome constructive criticism; those who like the idea of moving on but who balk at the work involved are less likely to be positive about it. But some folk who are keen to serve the Lord have yet to receive the healing necessary to enable them to cope with even minor criticisms; they're still so insecure and vulnerable that anything remotely critical razes to the ground their low-level self-esteem and brings on a full-blown rejection crisis.

It's not possible to deal here with the complexities of all the issues involved, but it's important to recognize that we are unwise if we seek to build up fragile brothers and sisters in Christ by giving them major responsibilities in the church. If someone is unable to cope with any negative comment, however lovingly motivated and delivered, it's foolish to put them in charge of a major area, for example, the music or pastoral care. They risk being devastated if feedback is not wholly positive; the church may suffer if constructive dialogue is impossible. It's far better to arrange for vulnerable men and women to work as team members, with more modest within-team responsibilities, supported by others. As their self-esteem evolves along biblical lines, and trust is developed and reinforced, greater responsibility may well be appropriate.

Yes, we must build one another up. Yes, this will involve encouraging people to use their gifts, perhaps in new ways and with an element of risk—but not rashly over-extending them way beyond their emotional, spiritual or practical capabilities, recklessly exposing them to the consequences of failure. Yes, criticism can be a valuable part of the refining process within the body of Christ when it truly is done in *agape*-love, and is given and received in the context of supportive, nurturing relationships.

Confronting sin and temptation

Confessing our sins to God is a form of self-criticism, although obviously there's a lot more to it than that. It's a necessary discipline for all Christians, especially when sharing the Lord's Supper (1 Corinthians 11:28), so that we can be made clean by God before we receive the bread and the wine. In addition, confession of sin may be part of growing up and moving on. As Esther de Waal says, 'Maturity comes only by confronting what has to be confronted within ourselves.' She recommends a question posed by Sister Joan Chittister: 'In the last three things that bothered me in this community, whom did I blame?' (*Seeking God*). If difficulties are always someone else's fault, we need to ask the Lord to open our eyes, both so that we may come to him in confession and repentance and also in order that we may move towards maturity.

Confessing sins to each other

'Confess your sins to each other and pray for each other so that you may be healed' (James 5:16). Our response to this verse is likely to be conditioned by our attitude to formal confession to a priest, but this isn't what James is writing about. He's visualizing the parts of the body of Christ in the normal course of their relationships. 'Confess your sins to *each other*,' he says. And note in passing that the context supports the view that confession of sin may have a part to play in healing prayer (see also Psalm 32:1–5).

Some confession of sin to one another will come in the context of asking for forgiveness from a person we've hurt or harmed; there may be no need to involve a third party. Sin that has directly or indirectly affected the church in a significant way should be confessed to a leader. He or she can then discern what needs to be done to bring cleansing and healing to the fellowship.

Obviously, we must be wise about which sins are confessed to whom and in what context. We must also avoid the snare of believing that our forgiveness is always dependent upon confessing to another person; it is not. When we ask God for his forgiveness, he gives it to us. But even when asking for their forgiveness isn't an issue, confession to another Christian may be helpful if, for example, we're struggling with feelings of defeat or grubbiness, or are coming under accusation from the Evil One. They can then remind us, maybe using 1 John 1:9, that God forgives those who repent, and pray prayers for our cleansing and protection.

Whatever the sin, the aim is—along with making any necessary reparations—to proceed to prayer for forgiveness and healing, and to draw a line under the matter. There is no reason to do the rounds of all and sundry with the same confession, unless we have wronged them all. Any tendency to wallow in the self-abasement of confession needs to be confronted firmly but lovingly, in order that the real issues (which may include self-hatred, possibly linked to past abuse) may be addressed.

Resisting temptation

Temptation is not the same as sin—Jesus was tempted but he did not sin—but being honest about our temptations can also be worthwhile. Temptations are by definition attractive to us: chocolate is tempting; cold, congealed porridge is not. Thinking more widely than food, we vary in what we find difficult to resist, but the Evil One knows our individual weak spots and requires no invitation to put them under pressure.

When the serpent sidles up to one of us and begins, 'Did God *really* say...?' (Genesis 3:1) we should be able to stand together and reply with confidence, 'Yes, he did!' If a few trusted friends know where we're vulnerable, they can help us not to gravitate from temptation into sin. We can ask them to pray for us and, if it seems right, to ask us from time to time how we're getting on in the area or areas we find difficult, as the battle for godliness goes on.

Martina, a Christian in her twenties, shared with me about a recent occasion on which she'd found herself strongly tempted to sexual sin. Recognizing the danger, she had extricated herself speedily. Martina was anxious about how I might react when she told me, but my response was affirmation: she had judged correctly that she needed to extricate herself—to flee temptation; she had managed her 'retreat' very well; she had learned her lesson. Martina had already made it clear that she had no wish to end up in that sort of situation again, and we were able to talk through some of the boundaries she could choose to put in place so that she didn't.

Resisting temptation may in some circumstances involve suffering —choosing to stay with the pain rather than taking the easy way out. This is particularly true in areas in which the world's standards are very different from ours. Our unwillingness to abandon biblical standards may provoke others to attack us or, at the very least, to think negatively of us. We have the assurance that Jesus is able to help those who are being tempted (Hebrews 2:18). Our heavenly Father will not let us be tempted beyond what we are able to bear, but will provide what we need in order to be able to 'stand up under it' (1 Corinthians 10:13). These verses are not specific about the type of help to expect, but although some of it will come through the strengthening ministry of the Holy Spirit, might not some of it also come through the Spirit-led support and ministry of the surrounding parts of the body of Christ—if we let it?

Pressing on

Paul wrote, 'Forgetting what is behind and straining towards what is ahead, I press on towards the goal to win the prize for which God has called me heavenwards in Christ Jesus' (Philippians 3:13–14). The past is by definition past, and some people misuse this verse of scripture to reinforce their view that it should be left alone. However, by the time he wrote this, Paul had already confronted his past as a legalist and a persecutor of the Church (as Philippians 3:3–4 shows). Had he not done so, how might his ministry have been affected?

Leaving the past behind

Sadly, there are circumstances in which the tentacles of the past invade the present and even threaten to envelop the future. If the past keeps intruding on the present, whether in the form of unresolved anger, depression, fear, guilt, emotional pain, unforgiveness or un-confessed sin, the only way to truly leave it behind is to face it in order to allow God access to it.

We can prayerfully encourage one another to seek healing or forgiveness, involving specialists as necessary. The tentacles of the past are sometimes obvious but, where they are not, unskilled 'digging' with the counselling equivalent of blunt instruments is to be avoided. Whatever the circumstances, I find it helpful to pray (silently, or out loud) that the Holy Spirit will bring to the surface those things which are, by God's grace, to be dealt with *at this particular time*. God is wise, and can be trusted, and his timing is perfect.

If we're really wanting to 'throw off everything that hinders' we'll need to confront any recurring patterns in relationships or in our discipleship which are holding us back. Others are usually better placed to observe such patterns than we are! If we're open to their input, they can raise any concerns about, for example, long hours worked or family relationships showing signs of disrepair, and help us to question what has been going on, before our health or family suffer too much. Are we brave enough to open ourselves to this sort of help from one or two close friends? Or brave enough to offer it if asked?

The overarching aim is to learn from the past, to bring peace (*shalom*) where there has been pain, and then to move on, not to dwell on the past for ever. Where the problem has been sin—ours or someone else's—it may have some enduring consequences, but in God's mercy much may be left behind. Even where scars remain, God is able to do far more than might seem possible. Some have found themselves wearing 'a crown of beauty instead of ashes, the oil of gladness instead of mourning, and a garment of praise instead of a spirit of despair' (Isaiah 61:3). This passage is precious to many who have suffered past sexual or other abuse but who have been set free and made clean, and are living their lives with a freedom they once thought impossible. (See also Psalm 103.)

Hopes and dreams

When life is hard going, it's tempting to say, 'Never mind, it'll all be better soon'—once this or that has happened, when everyone has settled down, once the Lord has ironed out the difficulties… But we have to commit ourselves to living 'in the now'; trying to cope by focusing on a trouble-free and harmonious future is escapism, even when it's presented with a deeply spiritual gloss.

Yes, God is in control. Yes, he answers prayer. Yes, we can trust him. But we're still fallen men and women, surrounded by other fallen human beings, living in a fallen world, and God has not promised us a totally cocooned existence. The future will be challenging—perhaps even more challenging than the past has been. Jesus was very straight with his disciples on the night before he was crucified. He did tell them to 'take heart' because he had overcome the world, but only after he'd warned them that 'in this world you will have trouble' (John 16:33).

Worldly dreams of living happily ever after are seductive and, in the case of advertising, deliberately presented in such a way as to allow them to slip under our guard. If these ideas have slotted into place in our thinking, we'll find it much more difficult to imagine the radically different future into which the Lord may be wanting to lead us. It's good to remind one another of the values that matter in God's Kingdom, as an antidote to the world's focus on material prosperity and, increasingly in this post-modern world, expectations related to self-fulfilment. Choosing to follow Christ has consequences: it restricts our personal liberty to live and to plan as we please. If we're serious about continuing to follow Christ and becoming more like him, we'll accept the consequent narrowing of our options; if we're not serious about following Christ, we probably won't.

As I write this I'm asking myself where, by God's grace, I expect to be in two or five years' time. In two, I hope to have this book in print, and to have some idea what the Lord has said is to follow it, as far as my writing work is concerned. In five, I expect to be in a period of change precipitated by my husband's retirement—he's already receiving junk mail urging him to plan for an idyllic future! In the case of the book, I've set a variety of goals (short-term, longer-term) covering the work I need to do before the date when I must send it off to the publisher. But I've also made a commitment to seeing my spiritual director, making space for reading and reflection and so on, because my relationship with the Lord is foundational to everything I do.

We can pray together about our hopes and dreams, and support one another in prayerfully setting goals that reflect God's purposes. But *our* goals must relate primarily to *our* lives. For example, when my children were younger, it would have been foolish to have as one of my goals that they would pass all their exams. Instead I made it my aim to provide a supportive home environment within which they could do the necessary study, and to be available so that they could talk through any concerns.

Some find the whole idea of hopes and dreams threatening because it raises the possibility of disappointment or failure. Carefully chosen goals may not be reached if unexpected circumstances intervene, so we need to be relaxed enough to revise them if it seems appropriate. But there's little point in having goals in the absence of serious intention. It's good to be alert to the possibility that our hopes have not been realized because, while we were happy to compile a 'wish list', the will to do the work involved was lacking from the start or quickly evaporated once the heat was on.

We can come alongside one another in the disappointment and pain of dreams shattered by circumstances beyond our control. We can also help one another to face reality when the responsibility for dashed hopes lies at least in part with us. The root cause may have been inexperience or lack of information—in which case we may already have learned something of value for the future. If the problem is a recurring one, others may be able to prompt us to ask the question 'Why?' Is there, for example, a destructive pattern of behaviour such as taking on numerous commitments, and then dropping everything at short notice when it all becomes too much? Are we in the habit of making unwise or undisciplined choices, such as choosing to take extra holidays when we can afford neither the money nor the time? If so, it will be necessary to reflect, and to ask for any help we need before moving on, if we're to do differently next time.

Changes ahead

Few of us find change easy to embrace. Even planned and eagerly anticipated changes, such as starting college, getting married or retiring from work, may be surprisingly unsettling. When several changes come along together, the overdose may threaten our well-being or health. At times of upheaval in our working, family or personal lives, and in times of natural transition such as adolescence, being part of the body of Christ can complement the stability we find through faith and trust in a God who holds our future secure.

It may be equally difficult to adjust to new roles in the body of Christ. If life-changes or advancing years are forcing men and women —temporarily or permanently—into being receivers when they have previously functioned as givers, this may bring a sense of bereavement or even feelings of loss of worth. Conversely, if the retirement of those who have always taken the major responsibilities leaves new hands holding the reins, this may feel scary all round!

Taking over from someone who has a lifetime of experience is daunting. If possible, it's far better to work together for a while, so that expertise may be shared while still in harness. But this requires a certain amount of forward thinking and a willingness on both sides to acknowledge that a move will happen in the medium or longer term. Where teamworking is the norm, this is less traumatic: the new leader is already working alongside the old, learning the ropes; the experienced worker is able to retire from their leadership role while still having much to contribute, remaining a much-valued member of the team—possibly for much longer than they would have been able to cope with if they'd borne the weight of responsibility right to the end.

Moving on, but not out

The truth that there's no retirement age in the Kingdom of God is little comfort if the one job you've always enjoyed is now beyond you! Some but not all of our most senior citizens adjust happily to the role of being 'just pray-ers' rather than 'doers'. My friend Elsie, now with the Lord, found it hard as she became increasingly immobile, but she didn't allow this to distract her from the opportunity to spend extended time in prayer. I shall always be grateful for the prayers she offered up for our sons when they were teenagers.

The psalmist says that the righteous 'will still bear fruit in old age' (Psalm 92:14)—and that was certainly true of Elsie. An elderly person who has lived a life of godly obedience will have acquired much wisdom along the way. (See, for example, Simeon and Anna, Luke 2:25–38.) If they've consistently offered themselves to God and allowed him to renew their minds, they're more than likely still equipped to 'test and approve what God's will is' (Romans 12:1–2). They may not be familiar with all the latest practices, but this doesn't mean they have nothing to contribute—quite the opposite! Fashions in theory and practice come and go, but true wisdom and discernment are always applicable. We need to ensure that older or physically weaker members are not involuntarily pensioned off, especially in a way that conveys an end to usefulness. The Evil One works hard to convince God's children that their lives are without significance. Let's make sure that we don't aid and abet him in this.

In contrast, those who have allowed themselves to be conformed to the world's pattern (Romans 12:2) and paid little attention to their relationship with their heavenly Father may find the increasing limitations imposed by age or infirmity deeply threatening. If their sense of being has been bound up in their 'doing' in a life brimming with busyness, 'stopping doing' can feel like 'stopping being'. What's more, an increasing awareness of their own mortality may precipitate a crisis of faith, made all the more traumatic if, while the church has been an ever-present feature of their lives, God himself has been distant.

Confronting our own mortality

Some statistics are viewed with suspicion, but here's one that everyone knows is totally reliable: sooner or later, physical death comes to one hundred per cent of people. The world's response is to spend time and money on anything that promises to reduce the evidence of advancing years. Our attitude should be distinctively different. Of course we'll want to do all we can to encourage one another to stay healthy, and to support those whose medical work is directed towards limiting or curing disease. But as members of the body of Christ we can also help one another to face and negotiate the inevitable changes that occur with age, or with serious illness at any age, and to confront our own mortality.

Confronting our own mortality isn't easy. I've been forced to do so on several occasions, for medical or other reasons, and I still find it quite difficult. I'm glad, however, that the Rector of our church reminds us from time to time in the course of teaching or conversation that we won't be around for ever, and speaks enthusiastically of heaven. The process of dying can be painful and unpleasant. Sudden and untimely death is traumatic for a whole community, not just the family of the one who has died. But if we belong to Christ, we have nothing to fear from death itself—if what we claim to believe about eternity has become a genuine part of the way we view life. I find the concept of eternity difficult to grapple with intellectually. It feels more manageable if I think of it in terms of an enduring relationship with God that will continue beyond death, growing stronger rather than weaker.

As part of moving on together, can we explore ways of strengthening that enduring relationship, gently challenging one another if we suspect that God is distant and that the hope of heaven is nothing more than an 'I wish' or a 'maybe'? Are we bold enough to remind one another, as Paul reminded his contemporaries, that this world is not our permanent home—that 'our citizenship is in heaven' (Philippians 3:20); that 'what is seen is temporary, but what is unseen is eternal' (2 Corinthians 4:18)?

Becoming

For some, especially the activists among us, thoughts of moving on are routinely translated into lists of yet more things to be done. If we're to move on, there *will* be things to be done. But given what I've just said about the importance of a renewed mind and an enduring relationship with God, perhaps even the activists will see that there's a need to reflect on issues relating to our inner life—something that many folk aren't inclined to do until they know they're dying and have little time left.

In addition to making time for reflection on the sort of relationships we're developing with God and with our brothers and sisters in Christ, we could ask questions like 'What sort of person am I becoming?' There is worth in the things we do, if they're done according to God's purposes, but the sort of person we are matters too. Are we giving God access to our inner being, allowing him to shape us, or are we crowding him out by filling our lives with worthy doings?

Think back to some of the words Jesus spoke to his disciples just before he died: 'If anyone loves me, he will obey my teaching. My Father will love him, and we will come to him and make our home with him… If a man remains in me and I in him, he will bear much fruit; apart from me you can do nothing' (John 14:23; 15:5). Do you think Jesus really meant it when he said 'nothing'? I think he did. Loving obedience, serving others, building the body of Christ, moving on to maturity—they are all dependent on an intimate relationship with God. The more we welcome God's shaping of our becoming, the more we allow Father, Son and Holy Spirit to set up home at the centre of our being, the more we'll become the godly, fruitful people God intends us to be.

Focus Point

- What type of race am I running? Whom have I chosen, consciously or unconsciously, as my training partners? Or have I chosen to avoid partners? If training partners don't appear to be available, make this a matter for prayer. God might reveal options you hadn't noticed.
- What are my hopes and dreams? Do I want to set godly goals for my life (short-, medium- and long-term)? What is *really* important to me? Are there aims for which I'm prepared to 'throw off everything that hinders'? Not everyone will approach these questions in the same way. Those with more spontaneous personalities prefer to take things as they come and find thoughts of goal-setting tedious; those who prefer structure may dismiss all unforeseen opportunities as distractions! The good news is that God knows us better than we know ourselves. If we offer the future to him, he can lead us on in ways that dovetail with the way he has made us.
- Paul wrote to the Galatians, 'Brothers, if someone is caught in a sin, you who are spiritual should restore him gently. But watch yourself, or you also may be tempted' (Galatians 6:1). Are there people who could lovingly say hard things to me if the necessity arose? If not, would I like there to be...? Talk to God about your answers and your feelings about them, and listen to what he says.
- Am I becoming more the sort of person God intends me to be?

Further reading

Dallas Willard, *The Spirit of the Disciplines*, Hodder and Stoughton, 1996.
Hebrews 12:1–17.

8

We Who Are Many
Are One Body

In Christ we who are many form one body, and each member
belongs to all the others.

ROMANS 12:5

The way God designed our bodies is a model for understanding
our lives together as a church: every part dependent on every
other part, the parts we mention and the parts we don't, the parts
we see and the parts we don't.

1 CORINTHIANS 12:24–25, THE MESSAGE

I've written much about how we as individuals can love, serve and
encourage others, build and be built up, move on to maturity and so
on. This has been right and necessary from a practical point of view: the
only person I can control is myself; if I'm seeking to change the world
for God, the change needs to have begun with me. But this mustn't
distract us from the glorious truth that 'in Christ we who are many form
one body, and each member belongs to all the others' (Romans 12:5).

The truth of this verse of scripture first hit me right between the eyes
about thirty years ago. Simon, a fellow student who had just become
a Christian, was giving his testimony. He said that in the course of
making his decision to follow Christ he'd realized that the commitment he was making was not just to be joined to Christ but to be
joined to all of us too. This was said as an aside, but his words gripped
me—and they've stayed with me.

The body of Christ is made up of *inter*dependent—not *in*dependent—Christians; it's a unit built from interdependent parts —each doing their work, but functioning as one. Within the body of Christ the members have individual*ity*, but there is no place for individual*ism*. That's the biblical perspective. Cultural influences and our sinful nature may combine to cause us to prefer a different model, but that's the one we've signed up to!

Community life, body life

The Church worldwide is the body of Christ. However, the New Testament recognizes both our universal connectedness and our local assembly (*ekklesia*, 'church'), and in practice we usually apply the words 'body of Christ' to the Christians in our locality. I'll be concentrating on the body of Christ in the local church, but much that follows may be applied in a house group or other group setting. And in fact it's my experience that as local church communities apply the New Testament 'one-anothers', their attention turns outwards; the worldwide dimension is opened up, not neglected.

In ordinary communities there may be an awareness of the community being greater than the sum of its parts, but the body of Christ is a living entity whose life comes from God, so it goes beyond other communities in some important respects. First, we are members of the body of Christ because Christ is in each of us (Colossians 1:27) and each of us is 'in Christ' (Romans 12:5). Members can be members only because they *are* in Christ and have Christ in them. Membership presupposes a relationship with Christ the Head (Colossians 2:19); relating to the Head cannot be left to a chosen few.

Second, the parts of the body of Christ are 'arranged' together by God, 'just as he wanted them to be' (1 Corinthians 12:18). The body of Christ has been brought together by God: it's not a community founded upon human decision or brought together by human agreement; any views we may have on whom we would like (or not like) to be a member, and what part they should (or should not) be playing, are not as important as we might like to think.

Why bother with community?

Why bother? After all, the potential that human beings have for falling out with one another and causing friction—even outright war—is well known. Isn't the parallel line approach (going in the same direction, but without touching) safer, because it makes fewer demands of members and gives less potential for unedifying schism? Is 'connectedness' really worth all the time and trouble? And anyway, isn't it all just a passing fashion—jumping on the post-modern relationships bandwagon?

Whatever our views on post-modernism, if we want to follow Christ and live according to his instructions we have no option but to 'bother'. His summary of the commandments spoke in terms of loving both God and our neighbour (Matthew 22:37–40). The prayer he taught his disciples and which we still use today begins, '*Our* Father'; each time we pray it we place ourselves alongside all God's other children. What's more, the teaching on love that Jesus spoke and demonstrated on the night when he was betrayed is difficult to put into practice in holy isolation.

Paul's teaching on the body of Christ does not appear to allow for solo discipleship. Even those who for one reason or another are 'out on a limb', such as Paul himself at various stages of his ministry, are still connected. This brings both benefits and responsibilities. Paul makes it clear that God gives certain gifts to some members of the body, and a different mixture of gifts to others, so that no one member (even a church leader) has the capability to do everything; the parts of the body of Christ have been designed for interdependence. (See the comments on diversity and the related scriptures given in Chapter 1.)

One of the major reasons for building Christian community, other than obedience to biblical teaching, is the potential for displaying gospel principles on a large canvas. Communities in which core members have certain goals in common, and share and apply the same foundational values day by day, are a sign and a foretaste of the Kingdom of God. This will have a profound influence on those who view from outside as well as on those who have chosen to join.

Every Christ-like life acts as salt and light and makes an impact on the world around. But take a group of Christian men and women showing *agape*-love in action, living biblically, forgiving one another, serving and encouraging one another, building up and urging on, rejoicing with those who rejoice and mourning with those who mourn, relating to one another as children of light—can that be anything other than challenging? It has the potential to change the world! We aim to build up the body of Christ in order to provide a strong base for reaching out—into the neighbourhood, the office, the canteen, the launderette, the town council, the prison, the playgroup, the factory...

Too close for comfort?

Although the friction that closeness may bring isn't a reason for opting out, I'm sure we all have days when we'd rather be building a personal ivory tower than a community. Some fellow Christians can be so... well, impossible. Does the body of Christ really have to have such a large 'grumbling appendix'? How can we make anything resembling progress when all Sharon ever wants to talk about is saving the whale, and Shaun keeps asking, 'Is the football on yet?' All sport's like a red rag to a bull as far as Harold's concerned, but does he have to be so confrontational? And why does he have to stir the sugar into his tea for five whole minutes before he'll let the next person have the spoon...?

Within any close community we learn things about others, and about ourselves too—maybe things we'd rather not learn, such as how impatient we are, how quick to judge or how ready to take offence. It's not just our friends whom God uses to bring us towards greater self-knowledge: it's often our interactions with those whom we might wish to describe as our enemies (if we weren't so

'Christian'!) that force us to exercise the great Christian virtues and teach us the most enduring lessons.

If community life is new to us, we may be reluctant to be honest about what we find difficult, to reveal the fragile nature of our hopes and dreams. However, if others are prepared to be open with us, sharing their hopes and fears, pains and delights, we'll eventually learn that it's safe to risk being more open ourselves. But then one day they'll let us down by a careless word or an insensitive laugh, and we'll have to learn to forgive, and then to trust again. It's no easy road.

Community climate

A mature Christian can disciple a new believer; a mentor can provide a role model for a growing disciple; a counsellor can work with someone who is struggling through personal difficulties; a spiritual director can come alongside a child of God who is seeking to know their heavenly Father better. But the benefits of these special relationships are multiplied enormously if the person being discipled/mentored/counselled/directed is part of a fellowship (community) where the same values are being reinforced and the same disciplines are being practised.

Creating a healthy climate

The 'climate' I'm describing may sound rather like positive peer pressure, but I want to make a distinction: peer pressure usually relies primarily on fear—the fear of being out of step, of being found wanting by those whose opinion matters. God's plan is that women and men should be drawn by love, *his* love at work in and through the body of Christ. Should they choose a sinful path, the sadness of those around them may demonstrate something of how God feels when sin disrupts their relationship with him. But they need to know that God and the community members love them unconditionally, and to be drawn by that love—not by fear of disapproval.

The main advantage of being surrounded by a community demonstrating—however imperfectly—what is being learned, is that this underlines that it's not just fine-sounding theory which collapses once real human beings become involved! One-to-one modelling of how to apply Christian teaching is worthwhile, but the body-of-Christ community living as a visual aid, showing day by day how it works in practice, will be even more powerful. Study Session 8 (page 187) looks at some of what God has given us to help us with community life.

I've written of the value of mutual encouragement in living biblically, which includes a commitment to practising forgiveness—foundational to a healthy climate. A church family will also need to model dealing with other aspects of life and faith, especially those that might threaten to overwhelm an individual or family soldiering on in isolation. Facing a crisis of faith can feel more manageable surrounded by a small group of brothers and sisters in Christ, supported by the wider community. All will benefit from a climate of genuine openness in which difficulties, while not being broadcast in every detail, are acknowledged—and I do mean acknowledging our own difficulties, not gossiping about other people's. If efforts are made to keep all problems tightly under wraps in order not to discourage folk (or for whatever reason), those who do sin, doubt, fear or struggle in other ways may believe that they are the only one to do so.

Owning doubts

Doubts can feel like sticks of dynamite, threatening to blow the whole of our faith to smithereens. But if they're handled carefully within a stable community this doesn't have to be the outcome. Some people have apparently been discouraged by Christian leaders from thinking too much about their faith lest they ask difficult questions. Others have transferred to the Church attitudes learned at school in the days when it was less acceptable to challenge the teacher; they may imagine that questioning is frowned upon when it's not.

When my artist-friend Jenny became a Christian many years ago, she had lots of questions. She was discipled by a wise woman who helped her find her way, but Jenny was told that there were some 'tough' aspects of the Christian faith which she might need to 'leave on the side of her plate for the time being'. Her doubts were taken seriously—they were not dismissed, but neither were they seen as a sign of lack of faith or a cause for panic. Jenny says that, as time has passed, the Lord has graciously resolved the doubts she'd left to one side. She now corresponds with a number of Christians overseas who write to her with their questions, and she is able to pass on the wisdom and help she received as a young Christian.

Thomas has been called the patron saint of doubters. The story of his inability to trust the other disciples' testimony that the risen Christ had appeared to them, and Jesus' response to him (John 20:24–27), has formed the basis for many a sermon. Thomas was open about his doubts. Had he been less open, he might not have been able to move so swiftly to his declaration of faith: 'My Lord and my God!' (20:28). In encouraging one another to move on, we can use Thomas as a model of a healthy way of dealing with doubts.

Thomas wasn't the only one to have doubts. Just before the verses at the end of Matthew's Gospel which are known as 'the great commission', we read that the eleven disciples met Jesus on the mountain in Galilee and they worshipped him, 'but some doubted' ('held back', THE MESSAGE, Matthew 28:17). Jesus commissioned them all anyway! If in our communities the prevailing climate is that doubts, used constructively, can be stepping stones to greater faith, maybe we'll find that more men and women are prepared to own up to them.

Allowing God access to our fears

Some churches find anxiety and fear even more difficult to handle than doubt, but once again the scriptures provide a model. 'Don't fret or worry. Instead of worrying, pray. Let petitions and praises shape your worries into prayers, letting God know your concerns. Before you know it, a sense of God's wholeness, everything coming together for good, will come and settle you down. It's wonderful what happens when Christ displaces worry at the centre of your life' (Philippians 4:6–7, *THE MESSAGE*).

Even in life-threatening situations, King David refused to allow fear to take over his life. He kept God at the centre of his thinking. This helped him to cope with his circumstances. In Psalm 56:3 he wrote, 'When I am afraid, I will trust in you.' He then continued, 'In God, whose word I praise, in God I trust; I will not be afraid. What can mortal man do to me?' (v. 4). The psalm's heading tells us that David wrote it when he'd been captured by the Philistines. I'm not surprised he was afraid! None the less, he managed to move from '*when* I am afraid, I will trust in you' to 'I will *not* be afraid'. Can we learn from David's way of handling things? Can we encourage one another to express fears to God in prayer, so that frightening times draw us closer to God? If we're afraid to reveal our fearfulness, it won't go away. It may even make us ill.

Years ago when I was a GP, I saw lots of patients who were suffering from fear, which may be anything from anxious concern to sickening dread or quivering terror. It's an emotion, but our bodies are affected, too: if we're afraid, the adrenaline is flowing, we're jumpy, our heart is thumping—our whole being is affected. God made us this way when he created us. When our well-being is threatened, for example by a lorry careering in our direction, fear puts our physiology into action mode. That gives us extra power to jump out of the way. The emotion of fear works with our bodies, enabling us to put some distance between ourselves and trouble. However, this life-preserving response is harmful to our bodies if it's triggered hour after hour, day after day, week in, week out. And if we're always being put on edge by pumping adrenaline, we may arrive at an 'anxiety state' in which the fear isn't just a feeling, it's a state of being; it isn't keeping us safe, it's tearing us apart.

In 1984 I learned first-hand just how disabling fear can be after a near-miss car accident. I'd chauffeured a friend to a hospital appointment. Afterwards, we were driving to collect our children from school when I saw a gas van on the wrong side of the road about 200 metres away, travelling very fast and coming straight towards us. I tried to work out what my options were. Should I pull on to the pavement? I was about to take avoiding action when the van suddenly swerved back to the right side of the road, missing us by a few feet.

It turned out that the driver had been drinking, and had killed a motor-cyclist before he came close to killing us. I coped with the immediate crisis, but life then became quite complicated. Having previously driven to work in London, I now drove as little as possible. If anyone's car wheels looked as if they were going to stray over the centre line in the road, I was halfway to taking avoiding action. I started to go to work by underground train. I felt acutely anxious the day I came home to find a gas van parked outside my house! I suppose these days I'd have been diagnosed as suffering from post-traumatic stress and offered counselling, but back then I was just left to get on with it.

The church we belonged to at that time offered prayer after the services. One evening I felt the Lord prompting me to ask for prayer. I can't remember what was prayed, but I do know that I turned a very big corner and was able to drive to work again. As I continued to pray that the Lord would heal the effects of the near miss, I got back to being able to drive without anxiety and stopped being allergic to gas vans. The fear that had been warping my life was no longer in charge— God was. As I put my trust in him, I was able to get back to normal.

Not all fears are trauma-based. Some are apparently unfocused yet blight people's lives. Sometimes medical help is necessary but, whether or not this is part of the answer, we need to model 'allowing God to be God'. Giving him access to our fears won't necessarily revolutionize the situation—although it may do. But choosing to trust brings a very different perspective: it takes fear off the throne and puts God in his rightful place. And it opens a channel for him to pour in his strength, to show his power, whether to change the circumstances or to enable us to come through them in a way that glorifies him. If we live like this, we'll become more effective in taking the message of good news and of a God who can be trusted to a needy and fearful world.

'In your anger do not sin'

This quotation (Psalm 4:4), used in Paul's letter to the Ephesians (4:26), reminds us that anger is often associated with sin, or is at best only a hair's breadth away, so it's no surprise that Christian communities prefer not to have to deal with outbursts of it. Righteous anger does exist—Jesus demonstrated it when the Jews tried to use a man with a shrivelled hand to catch him out (Mark 3:5). More often than not, though, our anger is the common or garden unrighteous sort that wells up, for example, when our self-will has been opposed or frustrated. Even anger that started out as righteous can degenerate rapidly if our sinful nature comes into play and we begin to take an unholy delight in the drama of it all.

Within the body of Christ it's best to take note of anger, and to consider prayerfully how to respond. Turning a blind eye and hoping the angry person will get over it may sound diplomatic, but we won't take this approach if we truly have their best interests at heart. If the anger is righteous, they may be needing our support, or even our assistance in pursuing an end to injustice or the righting of a wrong. If the anger is unrighteous they'll be needing our prayers, and perhaps also other forms of help. Encouragement and support can be offered as they come to God and ask him to show them his perspective on whatever has made them angry. It takes a lot of courage to draw alongside someone who is blazing with anger, but we need to ask the Lord how he would have us respond, resisting any inclination to 'pass by on the other side'.

Over the years, I've greatly valued those who have stayed close when I've been angry. They've helped me to take a step back and review things. Many times they've stopped me from falling into sin—or deeper into sin—when the hullabaloo of my anger was in danger of drowning out God's voice. Those who have helped least are those who have fastened on to my anger and used it as a vent for their own. Also unhelpful is earnest exhortation not to be angry—as if such a powerful emotion could be turned on and off at will! The most worthwhile course is usually to listen carefully and to reflect back to the angry person what is being heard—so that they can hear themselves more clearly (an example of 'reflecting' is given in the appendix, pages 159–160), meanwhile praying that God will give wisdom about how to proceed.

For many, the preferred approach to dealing with anger will continue to be to cover it over—to bury it. Unfortunately, buried anger is usually just as alive and dangerous when dug up years later, and may even wreak havoc while still 'six feet under'. When I counselled folk who were suffering from depression, it was not unusual to find a reservoir of unexpressed or unresolved anger fermenting beneath the surface of their troubled lives. Facing and dealing with our anger feels risky—but that's where a supportive community comes in. However, if anger is an established part of life, seems to go back a long way or feels very unsafe, it's usually best to work with a trained counsellor or therapist. Friends may not be equipped to handle deep roots, such as previous emotional or sexual abuse, if they emerge as part of the healing process. In such circumstances, friends are usually best kept as just that—supportive friends—while others take responsibility for the counselling.

The bottom line is that 'man's anger does not bring about the righteous life that God desires', as James warned his dear brothers in Christ (James 1:20). Whether or not our anger is justified, it provides a foothold for the Evil One. We need to support one another in bringing it to God, asking him to reveal any sin and to bring cleansing and healing.

Too painful for some

Having written that we must aim to build church communities where the likes of sin, doubt, grief, fear and anger may safely be dealt with rather than buried, I should add that if we do follow this course some will want to leave. This is because they fear openness; they are terrified that if they begin to lift the lid on what is within them, they and those around them will be seriously damaged.

People like this have a tremendous amount of unresolved

emotional pain. We must be merciful and gentle with them. If it's possible to keep supporting them within the community while they find the help they need, that's great. If they're willing to be befriended, that's even better. If we can continue to affirm (by our actions, not just our words) that we see them as precious children of God and accept them as our brothers or sisters in Christ, that will contribute to their healing.

If they choose to go, we mustn't receive that as a rejection of the community—it's not; we must allow them to leave on as good terms as possible, so that the way back remains open. We can urge them to seek fellowship with God's people elsewhere, and continue to pray for them. When meeting them, we can greet them warmly as our sisters or brothers in Christ. And if all this sounds too difficult, we can pray for grace!

As part of encouraging folk to seek healing rather than decamping every time they feel threatened, it would be good if more church leaders were prepared to risk taking an interest in the circumstances of those who join their church from elsewhere, asking what prompted the move. It's not a matter of passing judgment on who was in the wrong if there were disagreements. It's about facilitating cleansing, healing, learning and moving on—or indeed moving back, if the Lord so leads—once painful issues have been brought into the light and dealt with.

Love—the distinctive characteristic

Jean Vanier tells us:

A community isn't just a place where people live under the same roof; that is a lodging house or an hotel. Nor is a community a work-team. Even less is it a nest of vipers! It is a place where everyone—or, let's be realistic, the majority!—is emerging from the shadows of egocentricity to the light of a real love.

COMMUNITY AND GROWTH

Jesus emphasized the importance of love on the night when he was betrayed. The elderly apostle John would talk of little else. Peter told the Colossians, 'Most of all, love each other as if your life depended on it. Love makes up for practically anything' (1 Peter 4:8, THE MESSAGE). Chapter 3 looked at love in detail. However, the message bears reiterating here because without love, life in any community may become a matter of bitter endurance.

God-given *agape*-love is required both to keep a Christian community together and to keep it sweet. Moreover, the presence of love in a Christian community, along with the other aspects of the fruit of the Spirit (joy, peace, patience, kindness, goodness, faithfulness, gentleness, self-control), is a sign that it is the body of Christ, not just any old gathering.

Working towards community

Beyond loving one another as if our lives depended on it, what can we do to develop real community and 'body-life' in our churches? Start with this: 'stop, look and listen'. See what's happening. Listen to what's being said. Pick up on what's important to brothers and sisters in Christ and to the wider world. Take time to seek God's perspective on it all. If we begin in this way, we'll soon find that we're co-operating with what God is doing, and reinforcing good things that are already happening that we hadn't noticed! We may also become aware of the concerns of others which had previously passed us by and, because God is faithful and speaks to those who are ready to hear, we'll know more of his concerns and priorities.

Lest anyone assume that the stopping, looking and listening can be ticked off after a few hours of dedicated listening followed by a period of inspired reflection, let me make it clear that the intention is for this to become a continuing discipline, an aid to keeping the developing community in good repair. Some will take to this more easily than others on account of their personality or their gifting. But if we're serious about playing our part in strengthening the body of Christ, we can all ask for God's help in developing a greater awareness of what's happening and how he sees things.

Making time for communication

Good communication doesn't just happen. Work is required to keep the channels open—paying attention to what is communicated verbally and in other ways, whether or not it's agreed with or to be acted upon. It may be stating the obvious, but time is a necessary ingredient of this work; while most would agree in theory that this is so, some behave as if it were not.

An area that's worth exploring as part of the communication-building process is that of expectations. Try using the following questions:

- What are your expectations of me?
- What are your expectations of our community?
- What are your expectations of God?
- What are my expectations of you, of our community and of God?

Some of the conflicts arising within churches and other groups are the result of members having (often unexpressed) widely differing expectations of one another, of the community and of God, and also having made different guesses about what others, the community and God expect of them!

For example, if asked to summarize in thirty words or less what God expects of Christians, what would you say? I set this as an exercise for some groups, most of whom had worked together before, providing a few scriptures to get them started. A thirty-word answer forces a focus on the essentials. There were some difficult choices; not everyone's preferred phrases could be included. Some people accepted this more graciously than others. A few found the idea of not including everyone's view quite stressful. A number of participants were sure that a specific reference to walking in the power of the Spirit was essential; others wanted to emphasize belief, obedience or relationship. In some groups, the atmosphere rapidly became highly charged. Later, I asked everyone to reflect on how the decisions about the answer had been taken in their group—whether they or other group members had been heard (had some chosen to remain silent?) and so on.

If we're serious about ensuring that all parts of the body of Christ are able to function, and about strengthening the community life of our churches, these are the sort of questions we'll want to keep in mind in everyday settings, not just in exercises. And we'll want to check out from time to time the expectations that are building within our communities. Some of those expectations will have to be gently realigned with reality; others to be dismantled before they become set in concrete by the passage of time. It's good to have expectations of God and of one another, and to recognize that God and others have expectations of us—but let's make sure the expectations are biblical, rooted in truth.

Making time for fellowship

In some Christian circles it might be possible to come to the conclusion that 'fellowship' was a code word for tea and biscuits! In fact, the Greek word *koinonia* ('participation'), usually translated 'fellowship' (sometimes 'communion'), covers a broad sweep. It's used to refer to what we may all share because of the death and resurrection of Christ our Saviour, but it also relates to some of the vital intangibles of the Christian life—partnership, companionship, sharing and communicating. One tangible outworking will be sharing bread and wine together at the Lord's Supper, but Holy Communion or another form of church service was never intended to be the sole expression of *koinonia*.

Our church family chooses to make time for meals together in order to enjoy meeting in a more relaxed and unstructured way than is possible in services or over the tea and coffee afterwards. Most housegroups share a meal occasionally, as a way of developing their relationships and enjoying conversation without the limitations imposed by their normal style of meeting. One Sunday each month, everyone who would like to do so, and whose family situation permits, brings their lunch to the church hall, where we tuck into an interesting assortment of food. This provides a great opportunity to meet those from other parts of the church family and to include those who have not yet had the opportunity—or the courage—to join a housegroup. It's also an occasion for sharing hospitality with strangers who turn up in church on that Sunday, and with any non-church friends whom members care to invite.

Some of the men of the church meet occasionally on a Saturday morning for a cooked breakfast. After the meal, one of them shares the story of how they found faith or how the Lord has helped them meet life's challenges. From time to time there's also a 'men only' outing to the local bowling rink, followed by picking up a takeaway and reconvening at someone's home. (Bowling and a takeaway are comfortable options in a seaside town; men in other locations might wish to make different choices for an evening out.) These occasions provide opportunities for men to encourage one another and to bring along friends who don't normally come to church. They share the enjoyment of the meal and the company of men from all walks of life, while learning that faith is something that could make a difference in the situations they face from day to day.

In alternate months, newcomers to the church are invited for Sunday lunch at the rectory, followed by an informal presentation about our structures, values and activities and an opportunity to ask questions. We like to think that by the time people join the church they know something of what that means—what we might expect of them, and what is on offer in terms of ministry, pastoral care, prayer support and so on.

Maybe you're beginning to wonder if, in our church, 'fellowship' is a code word for a slap-up meal! Well, not exactly. Much sharing of fellowship goes on in a non-organized and unstructured way, for example in members' homes. And not all of it involves food and drink. Clearing out a basement together, performing or watching drama, transporting second-hand furniture to a new owner or sharing a good joke together can all be expressions of *koinonia*. But we've certainly found that food has an important place. Sharing a meal together facilitates genuine meeting but without feeling like 'a meeting'. Jean Vanier stresses that 'if a community is to forge its unity, its members have to be able to meet as people, as brothers and sisters, and not just as "job-doers"' (*Community and Growth*).

Demonstrating theory in practice

As part of being a community, we make a habit of marking significant milestones together. A fortnight ago, the 130th anniversary of the dedication of our main church building was mentioned. Last Sunday, we were delighted to note in our news-sheet that it was the 61st wedding anniversary of long-standing members Tom and Renée. There was another paragraph giving the names and destinations of teenagers heading to other parts of the country for university or training. Also last Sunday, we commissioned those who serve in the youth and children's work in the parish, as part of the main service. We then had a few words from Jenny (a nurse) and Kim (an occupational therapist) who were flying off to South Africa and Ecuador respectively on short-term missionary work.

Our weekly news-sheet includes requests from members of our three congregations with particular prayer needs. We try to remember to include thanks for answered prayer too, to give glory to God and to spur us on as we intercede. The names of those who are undertaking the Bible readings and leading the prayers are listed, which, especially in the larger congregation, acts as a way of putting names to faces. There may be a note of thanks to those who have run a special event or relinquished a role after a period of faithful service. Their doing it for God in *agape*-love doesn't mean that we can't say 'Thank you'. The news-sheet carries the usual range of notices about forthcoming meetings and activities, but it's important that there's more to it than that—just as it's essential that church life consists of more than one meeting after another.

Taken separately, each of these details of our church life is pretty inconsequential. However, taken together—the marking of comings and goings, the putting of names to faces, saying 'thank you', the public prayer support for members who are in need or who are 'out on a limb' in foreign parts, the sharing of significant anniversaries—they underline our spoken teaching that 'we who are many form one body, and each member belongs to all the others' (Romans 12:5). There's no point in preaching this if all the visible evidence would suggest otherwise.

Community leadership

Before considering the place of community leadership, we must consider how to recognize a leader. Our parish spent many months studying the nature of leadership in the body of Christ in preparation for choosing its first eldership team. We looked at Bible passages describing, among other things, the behaviour standards expected (for example, 1 Timothy 3; Titus 1:5–9). In addition, we observed the way leadership worked in practice around us, identifying many men and women within our three congregations who exercised leadership.

Discussing leadership with Vineyard church leader Matt Hyam, I was given the pithy definition used by John Wimber: 'A leader is someone people follow.' How true! Matt went on to emphasize that it's a matter of *recognizing* leaders—those who are already exercising leadership; those who are already following the lead of God's Spirit and are helping others to do so, whether or not they have an official role.

This style of definition serves to highlight the fact that within any community there may be individuals who are giving a lead that is *contrary* to the overall direction or ethos. When a church or a Christian organization considers appointing someone to a leadership role purely on the basis of the skills gained as a leader in a professional or other sphere, alarm bells should ring: a skilled leader can divert a church from God's purposes in no time at all.

Growing leaders

In our church, we try to ensure that leadership abilities are nurtured regardless of age. For those with leadership gifts, exercising them is part of moving on in obedience at any stage in life—leadership doesn't have to be grey-haired. As with other gifts, learning to exercise them will contribute to spiritual growth and development. We've benefited from having church council members in their late teens, twenties and thirties as well as the more usual forty-plus contingent. 'Don't let anyone look down on you because you are young,' wrote Paul to his son in the faith, Timothy, 'but set an example for the believers in speech, in life, in love, in faith and in purity' (1 Timothy 4:12). Leading by example adds credibility at any age.

If God is giving the necessary gifts to the many, there's no logic in leaving all leadership responsibilities with the few. For example, in our church two members of the eldership team co-lead one house group, but the remaining groups have non-eldership leaders. In any given year, church services will have been led by a couple of dozen members, aged from teens to seventy-plus.

If this sounds surprising, and unattainable in your situation, it may encourage you to know that few of those involved would have thought of themselves as capable of serving in such ways ten, even five, years ago. The unlocking of the gifts of these and other members of the body of Christ has come only after many years of faithful teaching on 'every-member ministry', and as a result of our current rector having the gift of spotting what women and men could be doing if only they had the courage and the opportunity.

The role of leaders

This brings me to the question, 'What are leaders for?' I use the plural here deliberately, as plural leadership is the New Testament pattern for the Church. The answer must be, 'It all depends…'. The specifics of leadership will vary depending on the nature of the situation and the gifting of individual leaders. In broad terms, the role of leaders is to keep the God-given vision before the community, reminding those being led of their destination and of the goals to be pursued and the values to be lived in the process of getting there. Good leaders do their best to ensure that, as far as possible, everyone is owning the vision rather than passively accepting it. Passivity in those being led raises serious questions about the leadership; an expert culture in which leaders are regarded as infallible and to be followed without question is dangerous for all concerned.

In practical terms, a key function of leadership is to facilitate the use of the gifts of all the members, so that each part *can* do its work (Ephesians 4:16). The equipping of all the saints for all the work of ministry to which they are being called usually requires a willingness to step back on the part of the leaders, so that others may gain experience. Let me say this unequivocally: leaders who feel threatened by gifted church members and who respond by trying to 'keep them down' have lost the plot.

Gilbert Bilezikian has written, 'The highest attainment achievable by leaders is to reproduce their expertise in "ordinary" people and to turn them into leaders. This is also the best expression of servanthood: leaders who train others to excel beyond them.' He goes on to say that John the Baptist's words about Jesus—'He must become greater; I must become less' (John 3:30)—could be taken as a servant leader's motto, adding, 'Servant leadership is to empower others to become greater than oneself.' Bilezikian has likened servant leadership to 'the work of a patient coach, who discovers the potential talents of team members and enables them to take the field while cheering for them from the sidelines' (Gilbert Bilezikian, *Community 101: Reclaiming the Local Church as Community of Oneness*, Zondervan, 1997).

Leading values

'Do as I say, and not as I do' is a poor strategy for leadership in any context, and has no place in a Christian community. Walter Wright, President of Regent College, Vancouver, warns that 'people tend to live out the culture that they have been part of rather than the values that are articulated by the leadership' (Walter C. Wright, *Relational Leadership*, Paternoster Press, 2000). Wright goes on to urge leaders to examine the cultural values they are reinforcing, possibly unwittingly, by their lifestyle and behaviour.

Leaders must be able both to articulate and to demonstrate the values that their community holds dear. They can't do this if they haven't been around long enough to know what those values are. In our parish, only those who have completed or are in the process of completing the 'Called to Serve' course are able to take on leadership roles. Those who go on to make effective leaders are usually happy to spend time settling in, getting to know the way things work locally, forming closer relationships and serving the body of Christ in other ways, before taking on significant responsibility. In any case, I'm always uneasy when newcomers arrive bursting with enthusiasm for leadership roles and nothing else.

Leaders need to be prepared to challenge any unbiblical assumptions about the way things are done. For example, the world's way is to give preference to those with power, whether in terms of wealth, physical size or influential connections. Jesus confronted this sort of attitude in the Jewish leaders, both verbally (for example, Matthew 23:1–12) and by the way he lived and died. James was concerned about some of the attitudes he detected in the early Church, and pointed to a different way (James 2:1–4). 'Be devoted to one another in brotherly love [*philadelphia*],' Paul urged the Romans, continuing, 'Honour one another above yourselves' (Romans 12:10). Leaders who model such teaching will be blessed by the resulting climate.

The valuing of diversity needs reinforcing by the leadership, lest individuals who stand out in any way are seen as a threat. A human body is seriously handicapped if something as small as a thumb is missing, and the body of Christ also needs the full range of God-given diversity to be in place. In addition to having been given different gifts, we've been created with differing personalities and styles: we dress differently, we learn differently, we pray differently, we worship differently; some revel in spontaneity and enjoy the unexpected, yet others prefer community life and worship to be organized and reasonably predictable; some readily grasp the commitment involved in being a disciple of Christ, while others lay hold of the tremendous freedom he brings; some are aware of that which is real but unseen (2 Corinthians 4:18), but where would they be without the faithful attention others give to the visible and tangible. Truly we need each other!

It's important for church leaders to value all the members—and not just for what they do or give. Yes, really! *All* of them—including those whom the world's communities may prefer to exclude. If leaders are seen to be welcoming, that will bring glory to God as well as enriching the body of Christ. In addition to being a part of the body of Christ with a role to play, each man, woman and child is a child of God who bears his image (Genesis 1:27). What could be more precious than that?

A work in progress

You probably know the old joke that says, if you find the perfect church you shouldn't join it, because then it would no longer be perfect. The church to which I belong isn't perfect—far from it! We aim to follow the Lord's leading, but we do get it wrong. Sometimes we get in a muddle, and sadly we sometimes hurt one another. 'Living on a building site' just about sums it up. The body of Christ is a work in progress. It will remain so until Christ comes again.

As with our personal circumstances, so in any community it's easy to fall into the trap of thinking that when we've survived the present crisis, community life will be wonderful. Not so! Idolizing the idyllic future we'll enjoy together when the current problem is resolved is dangerous. Worldly optimism so easily displaces the true virtues of hope and faith. It's more a matter of reaching the stage of maturity as a community, such that crises and unsolved problems no longer threaten to blow the community apart... and then living through them as they continue to arrive.

Making progress together is usually hard work, but leaders have an even more difficult job if their church community prefers standing still to progressing. How can they respond to a culture in which the only role anyone wishes to play is that of spectator, and saints are less than enthusiastic about being equipped? A long-term view is essential: don't focus on what *isn't* being achieved in the short-term. Preach and teach faithfully and persistently about the body of Christ as described in the New Testament; build up actively and intentionally—even those who are being unhelpful; model shared leadership and servanthood at every opportunity. Then, when everyone has had time to absorb some of the new values and ways of doing things, and the Lord confirms that the moment has come, press on—prayerfully, gently, lovingly—in obedience to his will.

Growing pains are a sign of growth!

As you've read this book and reflected on the life of your Christian community, I hope you've been able to see that God has been at work, in you and in others. I hope that you'll have been encouraged to press on. I pray that the Lord will lead you to others who are like-minded—if you haven't already found them. At times, community growing pains may feel overwhelming; you may be tempted to quit. The chaos of eyes, elbows, toes and tonsils trying to work together for the common good in the body may generate frustration, even despair. Pray that the Holy Spirit will enable you to see beyond the chaos to the tremendous potential for fruitfulness, and to share something of the vision Paul had when he enthused about the body of Christ with its diverse parts all those centuries ago. And pray for love such as you've never before been able to share.

The primary task of the body is to incarnate Christ in a desperately needy world—corporately serving, loving, caring, revealing, making known. May God bless you as you play your part.

I pray that out of his glorious riches [God] may strengthen you with power through his Spirit in your inner being, so that Christ may dwell in your hearts through faith. And I pray that you, being rooted and established in love, may have power, together with all the saints, to grasp how wide and long and high and deep is the love of Christ, and to know this love that surpasses knowledge—that you may be filled to the measure of all the fulness of God. Now to him who is able to do immeasurably more than all we ask or imagine, according to his power that is at work within us, to him be glory in the church and in Christ Jesus throughout all generations, for ever and ever! Amen. (Ephesians 3:16–21)

Further reading

Gilbert Bilezikian, *Community 101: Reclaiming the Local Church as Community of Oneness*, Zondervan, 1997.

Appendix: Listening Skills

Listening to one another is of immense value. Let's not imagine that unless we've contributed wise words or helpful advice we've 'done nothing'! Dietrich Bonhoeffer wrote, 'Christians, especially ministers, so often think they must always contribute something when they are in the company of others, that this is the one service they have to render. They forget that listening can be a greater service than speaking' (*Life Together*). In counselling circles it's a well-worn joke— not without truth—that Job's 'comforters' were doing fine when they sat in silence with him for seven days and nights (Job 2:11–13), but ruined it once they opened their mouths and started to speak!

Particularly now that prescribed counselling is in vogue, we must remember that it is an abuse of power to try to force troubled people to speak. This includes coercing them by telling them they're daft to bottle it all up because talking will do them good. Some research has appeared to demonstrate that *compulsory* counselling provided after major incidents, although aimed at reducing the incidence of post-traumatic stress syndrome, has for some individuals been counter-productive.

Voicing thoughts and feelings has value in many circumstances, including following a traumatic event, but—as with many other counselling issues—timing is a key factor. Some folk want to talk *now*. Others value being accompanied supportively but not intrusively until they're ready to speak. Some never feel ready, and we must remember that in such circumstances remaining silent isn't actually a crime.

Chapter 3 gave an introduction to the subject of listening, including a section on silence. This appendix covers more of the basics. The 'practice points' at the end and the exercises to be found in the group study section may be used to develop skills which are useful when listening to friends and family members. They aim to encourage listening to God, too.

I've also marked out some of the pastoral minefields into which good listeners wander simply because they are good listeners. This is to flag up potentially explosive areas, not to encourage unskilled digging. If you feel called to offer a ministry of listening, I strongly recommend that you enrol on a training course that provides opportunities for supervised learning and practice.

Conveying receptivity

If we know someone's coming to see us for a chat, it's part of general courtesy to check beforehand that there's somewhere suitable to sit and that our surroundings convey a welcome. If it's only after they've arrived that we remove piled paperwork from the chair for them to sit down, or switch off the TV thriller, they may pick up signals conveying busyness or a preoccupation with more interesting matters.

When meeting or welcoming those who don't know me well, I may greet them with a handshake. Touch is a powerful communicator, and shaking hands is a relatively non-threatening form of touch, but it's necessary to be sensitive: it will communicate different things depending, for example, on social background, and whether or not inappropriate touching has been part of a pattern of abuse. For some, a handshake is too formal; others may find it too threatening.

Where to listen

Sitting side by side on a sofa isn't ideal for listening, because it makes eye contact and the reading of facial expressions difficult. Comfortable chairs of a similar height are usually best, placed far enough apart to allow personal space but close enough to allow a sense of contact. Chairs angled towards one another are usually preferable to sitting directly facing, which can be a bit intimidating, especially if someone is nervous.

Sitting at a kitchen table together may work for more informal listening, but check that you're not using a table, or even an expanse of carpet, as a barrier. We probably all have memories of visiting a doctor or head teacher who took refuge behind a large desk and never seemed to connect with us, so it's best to try to avoid evoking that sort of situation.

The reality is, however, that significant listening doesn't just happen by appointment and in obviously suitable places. Don't despair—just do your best. Is it possible to gravitate to a more conducive spot without disrupting the flow? Sometimes the only option is to say, 'I'm finding it really difficult to follow what you're saying because of the noise/constant interruptions. I'd really like to be able to listen properly. Could we move to a quieter spot?' Or, 'Could we arrange to meet later/somewhere more suitable?'

Full attention

Whether our listening is prearranged or 'just happens', it's important not only to listen but to *show* that we are listening. If we're telling someone with our lips that we're listening, but our eyes keep darting over to check the clock on the wall, or we're endlessly fidgeting with our clothes or doodling on our memo pad, our words won't carry much weight. Yawning is one of the more obvious ways of conveying, 'I've had enough.'

While someone is telling their story, it's good from time to time to make friendly, non-invasive eye-contact (that is, not a penetrating stare). This says 'I'm with you.' The occasional nod, or some 'mms' or 'uh-huhs', will show we're paying attention to what's being said.

Having said all that about attentive listening, fragile folk may prefer a less intense style of encounter (with eye contact at a minimum) while trust is being built up. Sharing the washing up or taking the dog for a walk together are good examples. I remember as a teenager being listened to by a young mum while she worked through her mountains of ironing. I think I might have backed off if she'd immediately abandoned her ironing in order to 'listen properly'! The informal approach can be helpful provided it's used sensitively and carefully; informality isn't an excuse for sloppy listening.

Blocks to hearing

If we're intent on voicing our own point of view as soon as the speaker pauses for breath, this will act as a block to hearing and understanding. Even in informal discussions among friends, it's worth remembering that 'he who answers before listening—that is his folly and his shame' (Proverbs 18:13). I know my own weakness in this regard. I enjoy the stimulation of a good debate, and welcome the exchanging of ideas through animated discussion. It's easy to bring a debating approach into situations where it's unhelpful or even destructive. If a friend gets the impression that I'm only listening while waiting to reply, they're unlikely to feel fully heard or cared for. 'Lead with your ears, follow up with your tongue' is Eugene Peterson's wording of part of James 1:19 (THE MESSAGE).

Hearing may also be impaired by a sieving mechanism formed by our preconceived ideas and prejudices. For example, if we believe that real Christians don't get depressed, we may fail to recognize that a mature Christian friend is trying to tell us that they're feeling overwhelmed by gloom and hopelessness. If a friend is about to be married to someone we've decided is their ideal partner, we may dismiss any anxieties as pre-wedding nerves without really listening to what they have to say. It's up to them to decide whether or not their concerns are significant enough to affect their plans; it's up to us to act as a faithful sounding board—not a censor saying, 'You can't think/feel that.'

Hearing may also be blocked by physical or mental tiredness, and by distraction caused by our own needs, anxieties or illness. If we're aware on a particular occasion that attentive listening is beyond us, it may be best to explain that to the person who is trying to tell us their concerns, perhaps agreeing another time to meet. This will be more positive than leaving the person with the impression that we're not interested.

Whole-person listening

It would be easy to imagine that listening is just a matter of pinning back our ears. But speaking is much more than words. We need to draw information from the speaker's tone of voice, their fluency or hesitancy, and whether their speech drops to a whisper or climaxes in a shout at a particular point. We also need to listen to the whole person, not just to their voice.

Listening with our eyes

We 'hear' with our eyes as well as our ears. The speaker's facial expressions may speak volumes about the meaning and significance of what's being said. Their eyes (darting nervously? avoiding contact?) may indicate that the words being spoken—for example, 'Yes, everything's fine'—are some distance from the truth.

Body language more generally can be communicative. Try watching a TV discussion or soap opera with the sound turned off. In face-to-face listening, the overall level of physical activity, the body posture adopted—maybe changing as time goes on—and signs of physical tension or relaxation all aid interpretation of what's being said.

Some gestures speak a thousand words, although others are more a matter of habit or a sign of physical restlessness. It seems that less than ten per cent of what we communicate when speaking to one another comes directly from the words used—more than ninety per cent is picked up through the way we use our voices, our faces and the rest of our bodies. And remember, we all send out these signals all the time. Even if our voices are inactive while we're listening, our bodies are rarely silent. The person we're hearing may be 'reading' us and drawing their own conclusions. So, take care to avoid frowning or other facial expressions associated with disapproval—they may be triggered by our concern for the person who is speaking but could easily be misread.

Listening to God while listening to others

While putting our ears and eyes to good use in listening, we need to make sure that we're listening to God, too. Is he giving insights supernaturally, or prompting a particular question which will enable the speaker to open up on a deeper level?

The subject of listening to God is a vast one and, although it has been touched on at various points, to cover it in detail is beyond the scope of this book. Perhaps the most important thing to realize is that if we're to hear God while listening to others we need to be comfortable with hearing him at other times as well. If you're aware that you find hearing God difficult, consider asking for help from others in the body of Christ who are more experienced in this area. Look at the books and other resources available. Make it a matter of prayer. It's the sort of prayer God loves to answer!

Helping people to hear themselves

A vital part of the training of those in the listening professions is teaching them to enable their clients to hear themselves—to recognize and to acknowledge their own thoughts and feelings, their hopes and fears. In discussions with our friends it's normal to respond to their point of view or to their experiences by sharing our own, but there are times when it would be better just to listen. It can be helpful to speak briefly of our own experiences while remaining focused on listening to someone else, but there's a difference be-tween doing it for their benefit and doing it in order to have our say—or to brag about how well we've handled similar difficulties.

A mirror to thoughts and feelings

As an example, let's assume that Sally has just shared her difficulties with her child's class teacher. Rather than holding forth on the subject of troubles with teachers, we could act as a mirror to Sally's thoughts and feelings and say something like 'So, you're feeling angry at not being heard'—if that's what Sally seems to be saying. Sally can then consider whether the anger she is feeling is appropriately directed at the teacher, or whether she is in fact more angry with herself because she feels she's failed to express her concerns clearly.

Note that all the listener has done is to reflect back to Sally what she has herself expressed—through her words, her tone of voice and her body language. There has been no attempt to psychoanalyse Sally, her child or the teacher, or to classify her thoughts or feelings as right or wrong. Reflections gently offered can always be responded to with 'No, you've misunderstood'. Sally might, after all, want to respond by saying, 'No, I'm feeling angry at being brushed off as a fussy, interfering mother!' It doesn't matter that the first reflection was apparently inaccurate. Sally has now been able to articulate her concerns more clearly, which is usually helpful to the speaker as well as to the listener.

The listener could continue the mirroring by saying, 'So, the teacher has told you you're a fussy interfering mother?' Sally might go on to confess that the teacher has never said anything along those lines—it's just that she fears being classed as such. Such a fear may have led her to take the teacher's reassurances that there is nothing to worry about as a brush-off, confirming that he sees her as a nuisance. It's possible that if Sally has begun to approach the teacher with such thoughts in her mind, almost anything he says will serve to fuel her concerns.

'What am I telling myself?'

Our self-talk (the things we say to ourselves as we turn situations over in our minds, and the things we say to ourselves about ourselves) has a very powerful influence on the way we feel about events, and about ourselves too. If Sally is regularly telling herself that she's not a good enough mother, this will make her more anxious when dealing with her child's teachers. If she then goes on to tell herself repeatedly that she's hopeless at dealing with teachers, it's likely to become a self-fulfilling prophecy. This dynamic is repeated in all sorts of situations, and is responsible for much self-inflicted misery.

If we recycle untrue negative statements by repeating them to ourselves dozens (hundreds? thousands?) of times each day, the effects are bound to be destructive. Sally is unlikely to be a perfect mother, but she's probably a 'good enough' mother, and good teachers are prepared to accept the positive motives behind parental concern, even if they see it as unjustified. If the teacher's alleged view of Sally as a fussy, interfering mother is a product of Sally's fears, then recognizing it as such, and asking God for help with putting a check on any negative self-talk, may help her to move to a better relationship with the teacher.

Many Christians indulge in negative self-talk about God. 'He wouldn't be interested in me.' 'If I told God how I feel, he'd be angry with me.' Some Christians also tell themselves much the same sort of thing about church leaders and other authority figures, too. In spiritual terms, it amounts to doing the Enemy's undermining work for him. As part of listening to one another, it can be helpful to query any suggestion of this, to bring it into the light. Unfortunately, what sometimes happens is that a well-meaning person feels that the caring thing to do is to offer sympathy rather than a gentle challenge. This appears to legitimize the negative approach, allowing it to grow stronger.

Negative self-talk is usually more closely related to how people feel about themselves than to their experiences of God (or of teachers, doctors or church leaders). Either way, it's counter-productive in developing a relationship with their heavenly Father, and needs bringing into the light—to be lined up alongside what they *say* they believe, and alongside scripture.

Emotions while listening

If someone is sharing their hopes and fears, or expressing their pain and confusion, our own emotions will be stirred. This is part of being human; it's not normal to remain untouched by others' stories. However, if we're to be effective listeners we need to discipline ourselves sufficiently to allow the other person—for the duration of the listening—to have our full attention. If our own emotions hijack the focus, this will reduce our ability to listen attentively. When listening to a harrowing story, we may feel our eyes filling with tears. 'Is it wrong to cry?' I'm sometimes asked. It isn't 'wrong', and it isn't usually unhelpful, as long as the tears relate to the painful experiences of the person telling their story rather than to the buried, unresolved issues of the listener.

Painful times

There are acutely painful times in our lives when we know that our own emotions are too volatile to be contained. At such times we need to accept our limitations in terms of our ability to listen to others, and avoid taking on counselling-type roles requiring us to put our emotions on hold. Otherwise, if the men and women we're trying to help begin recounting painful experiences which resonate with our own pain—even if their experiences are unrelated to the source of our pain—this may be difficult for us. It may also be difficult for them if they are taken by surprise, having been unaware of our situation.

Organizations specializing in bereavement counselling do not normally take on counsellors who have suffered a major bereavement in the past year or two. This is not to say that friends cannot help and support one another in such circumstances—of course they can. It is simply that we need to recognize our own vulnerability and need for support at painful times. We do well to resist the urge to try to 'heal' others' pain as a way of distracting ourselves from our own.

Hearing ourselves while hearing others

Although our own emotions need to be held in check if we're to listen effectively, it's not helpful to squash them completely. They need to be noted, both for exploration later for our own well-being, and also so that we may use them, if appropriate, for the benefit of the person to whom we are listening.

While someone is telling their story, we may become aware of sadness, anger or another strong emotion developing within us in response to what we're hearing. If the person speaking is doing so without apparent emotion, this may be a sign that their emotions have been buried—usually because they're very powerful and feel too unsafe to acknowledge. If this seems to be the case, we must take time to consider whether or not this is the right time and place to enquire further, and whether or not we are the right person to do so. Buried emotions will usually keep—they're in cold storage—so there's time to respond thoughtfully, prayerfully, carefully.

Powerful emotions stirring in us as we listen could be a sign that we're about to get out of our depth. There's no need to panic! We can pray for wisdom to know how best to introduce the suggestion of looking together for additional help.

Difficult listening

Whether or not we set out to do so, from time to time we'll find ourselves hearing painful and disturbing things from fellow Christians. How we respond will affect not just us and the person we're hearing but also the wider body of Christ. This is particularly true when we're hearing criticism of leaders. Let me tell you a fictional story to illustrate what I mean.

Richard joined a church, having previously worshipped elsewhere in the same town. He let it be known that he'd left the other church after a serious breakdown in his relationship with the minister. Initially a willing volunteer in their youth work, Richard said he had rapidly felt over-extended. When he'd tried to express this, he'd not been heard. Richard saw the minister as unwilling to listen to anyone else's point of view. He'd decided that his only option was to leave. Now, however, he was happy in the new church and wanted to put it all behind him. He was glad after a month or so to be asked to help with the youth club.

Not many weeks later, the leader of the youth club and the minister tentatively broached the subject of possible changes to the way the club was run. Richard reacted very strongly. Clearly they weren't really interested in his views. They were planning to make sweeping changes which he could not support, so he might as well leave now.

The youth leader and minister didn't know what had hit them. A team consultation exercise had turned the club into a war zone. Not only was Richard threatening to leave, but his fear that plans were to be imposed had proved infectious— other members of the team were feeling unsettled and vulnerable. Disaster loomed. An urgent team meeting was convened so that the minister could respond to all the anxieties. Richard was sure that it was only a whitewashing exercise and didn't attend, sending his resignation letter instead.

The club leader was able to reassure the remaining leaders and helpers that nothing had been decided behind their backs. Eventually, after everyone had relaxed somewhat, the meeting turned into a useful discussion of possible ways forward. In the days that followed, Richard continued to maintain that the minister and leader were not really interested in input from others, and were planning to carry on with their hidden agenda. He soon left the church.

What has been going on? Is it that Richard's unfortunate experiences at the previous church have eroded his trust in leaders such that he's primed to respond fearfully and negatively as soon as he detects any plans afoot? Or is it possible that the root goes further back than that—maybe much further back? It could be that Richard responds in this way because much earlier difficult experiences with a parent, teacher or another authority figure have left him with unresolved anger and a 'certainty' that those in authority are unwilling to listen and not to be trusted. The body of Christ can be traumatized if listeners fail to recognize that pain, feelings and interpretations being expressed in connection with recent events may have originated much further back.

Distinguishing between feelings and facts

When listening to friends or other church members, it's helpful (whatever the subject) to try to distinguish between feelings and facts—and to encourage those who are speaking to do the same. If everything is taken as factual, it can cause havoc. Also, if you hear painful things about your leaders (or others), don't immediately assume that they are the whole and unadulterated truth. A lot of folk have difficulties with authority figures, and church leaders—especially kind, pastorally gifted men, as it happens—attract much undeserved blame as a result.

In any context, distressed men and women may be less than one hundred per cent clear in communicating what has happened, because distress *distresses*. This is not to be taken to imply that what they are saying should not be taken seriously—it most definitely should. But try to avoid leaping into action before going through the story to make sure you've grasped the real facts. Pause for careful consideration (unless there are reasons to suspect that someone is about to be harmed); most crises will keep for a few minutes and some for several hours or even a day or two while you pray for discernment and guidance.

In the story, Richard needed a friend who would encourage him to examine the facts, rather than to act on what he 'knew' was happening. Unfortunately, men and women like Richard have a tendency to move on and so lack long-term friends.

Leaders faced with this type of crisis need supernatural wisdom to know how to proceed. They also need to be determined to keep the channels of communication between them in good order, so that division cannot creep in. Allegations or inferences must not be allowed to assume the nature of 'fact' without being tested in the light of reality. If unwise or unrighteous things have been said or done, they must be dealt with biblically. The integrity of the body of Christ depends upon it. But a leader or other church member must not be expected to take the rap for something which has been perceived but which has no basis in present reality.

If as a leader you become aware that this sort of situation has developed, I suggest you pray earnestly for wisdom and consider seeking help or advice. Lack of trust is infectious. Pray for healing of the breach and that the Enemy will be unable to find opportunity in it.

Not attempting the impossible

All listeners need to know where to draw the line. I recommend that you review the sections on wise, loving listening and boundaries in Chapter 3. There are other issues that also need to be taken seriously.

Not having to know it all

If you're a good listener, you'll find that some individuals are keen for you to advise them on how to live their lives. Counsellors and spiritual directors are often perceived as professional advice-givers, trained to know the answer to everything. This is a complete misconception. It's important to understand this for two reasons. First, the notion of having to be the fount of all wisdom and knowledge discourages some highly suitable folk from taking up these roles—and it attracts the wrong sort of people, too. Second, it belies the amount of work that must of necessity fall to every counsellee and directee. Coming to a counsellor expecting to receive infallible advice might also be laying the foundations for, at best, disappointment.

Another misconception in Christian circles is that a spiritual director, and perhaps also a counsellor—especially if he or she is a church leader—is responsible for telling others what God is saying to them. Some folk are interested in hearing what God has to say; some are not. This applies to Christians as well as non-Christians. Some Christians do not expect God to speak; others fear that he might but would prefer that he didn't. All brothers and sisters in Christ need to encourage one another to hear God's voice, but that's a far cry from taking responsibility for knowing what God is saying.

Perhaps the key thing for any would-be helper to learn is that relatively few significant problems are easily fixable. What's more, taking over responsibility for others' problems doesn't usually help in the long run, as it deprives them of the growing experiences they would have had in the process of finding solutions to their own difficulties. Leaving aside the advisability or otherwise of taking over, I need to know *for my own sake* that I can't fix everything or everyone. Trained listeners are taught to keep their feet fully on the ground and to remember that they can't fix everything for themselves, let alone for everyone else. This isn't just because they're sinners and don't do everything right. There's an important sense in which this is true simply because they're human.

Knowing our limitations

Attentive listening is tiring work, and it's wise to limit the amount attempted in any one day or session. Forty minutes or an hour of quality listening, followed by an invitation to return at another time (or, in the case of informal listening, a transition to a less demanding activity such as preparing a snack together), is usually more valuable than pressing on for hours until everyone is worn out. Whatever the expected length, I make it a rule to keep free the time on either side of a scheduled session, in order to recharge my batteries.

If you've been told something distressing which is continuing to burden you and you're unable to lay it down, consider carefully who could assist you—preferably a trained counsellor, maybe in another church or another town. Accredited counsellors are required to be 'in supervision'. This means having another counsellor who helps them to monitor their practice and to cope with the impact of what they are hearing.

For this reason it's usually best to steer those with horrifying stories to tell towards those who are trained and equipped to cope and who are working within a framework designed to support their listening. This doesn't mean abandoning the troubled folk— you and others can still walk alongside them as friends, supporting them as they work through their pain, but aiming to build a more rounded relationship in which their difficulties are not always the focal point. This way, you'll be giving valuable support, but without carrying a greater load than you can bear.

As a listener, I know I need 'listening friends' myself—not to share the burden of what I'm hearing (my supervisor takes that role) but as caring friends. Having experienced much healing over the years, there are still areas in which I struggle and, although I expect to go on being healed, I don't expect to be fully healed this side of glory. I'm blessed with several good friends who know where I'm vulnerable. They will respond to a request for prayer, will expect an honest answer to questions such as 'How are you?' and will exercise my sense of humour when it's getting jaded. I strongly recommend that if you don't already have friends like that you make it a matter of prayer.

Further reading

Anne Long, *Listening*, DLT/Daybreak, 1990.

Joyce Huggett, *Listening to Others*, Hodder and Stoughton (second edition), 1996.

Practice Points

Being heard—or not

- Think of someone you regard as a good listener, and consider what makes them so.
- Recall an experience of not being listened to. What was it about this experience that left you feeling you hadn't been heard?

Body language

- When you're waiting in a queue, or have other free time in a public place, observe the interactions between people.
- What is their body language conveying? Are they listening to one another? If so, how are they showing it?

Hearing ourselves

- Towards the end of each day, spend a few minutes reflecting on events and encounters with people and your feelings about them.
- What was enjoyable?
- Did anything happen that 'pressed all your buttons' in a negative sense?
- Was there something you found particularly draining?

Hearing God

- Towards the end of each day, take a few minutes to bring the events and encounters, your feelings about them, and your reactions and responses, before God.
- Give God time to speak to you about your day. You may find it

helpful to keep a journal, both as an aid to reflection and as a record of what God says to you.

• As opportunities for listening arise, ask God to help you to cultivate the inner stillness which will enable you to hear more effectively what is being communicated—by him, and by others.

Group Studies

These sessions are designed for use in small groups, and will work best with six to twelve people. If you do not have a ready-made group, ask God to show you if there are folk with whom you could get together. The biblical teachings under consideration are difficult to put into practice working alone. You could make a start on your own, but I would urge you to persist in praying for at least one other person with whom to share them. It's good to establish ground rules before you begin, to help make the group a safe place in which to be open with one another. For example, you might choose to agree that nothing said in the group will be shared outside without permission.

Each session touches on issues raised in the chapter with the same number. The meetings will be more fruitful if at least the leader has absorbed the material given in the relevant chapter. At the start of each session there's a section for members to do on their own beforehand, in preparation. This is to encourage everyone to take some responsibility—for their own building up, for developing their listening skills, for contributing to the group. It is deliberate that there is no slot for 'testing on homework'. However, it would be good to allow a few minutes for covering any queries or difficulties arising from it.

Groups vary in their speed of working and in the time available. If your group is unable to cover everything, either leave out the 'further study' section or take two weeks over the material if your schedule allows. Each week, as part of encouraging one another, building one another up and growing in fellowship, you could ask a different person to share the story of their journey of faith—how they came to Christ, what has happened since and the various relationships they've seen God using to work out his purposes in their lives. If members have been Christians a long time, you'll need to set a time limit (for example, ten or fifteen minutes) and suggest they pick out key points along the way rather than telling the whole story—

otherwise there won't be time for a study. If time is limited, you may prefer to set aside a whole session for this purpose.

Some group members will warm to some studies or parts of sessions, and some will find others more helpful or enjoyable. If what you're working on at a particular time isn't really your cup of tea, look around for those who are finding it more worthwhile, and take care to listen to what they're getting out of it—that way, you may gain something, too. And even if you don't, you can thank God that they're benefiting.

Session 1

To prepare
Ask everyone to read 1 Corinthians 11:17—13:13 at home beforehand. See the context in which the teaching on the body of Christ is set.

The body in action

From the passage read beforehand, it will be obvious that Paul had concerns about the life of the church in Corinth. In the midst of expressing them, he began to teach about spiritual gifts. These are given to each one, by the one God, for the common good (12:4–7). Paul then went on to teach about the body of Christ.

Learning activity
Give out paper and pens/pencils. Ask everyone to write their name at the top of their piece of paper. Then ask them to write it again using their non-preferred hand. It may well be legible, but note the strain involved. Then suggest that they might like to try it once more, holding the pen with their teeth or their foot!

Offer someone with a sense of humour an individually wrapped biscuit or crunch bar. Tell them they may eat the contents—but only if they use their elbows to open it. When they protest that it's impossible, suggest that someone else could join in, also using only their elbows. Would this help? How might the biscuit fare? Two hands, each contributing a thumb and a first finger, might be better suited to the task.

Study time

Ask someone to read 1 Corinthians 12:12–31a out loud in the group. With the previous activities in mind:

• What does the passage teach about the body of Christ? You'll find it helpful to refer to Romans 12:4–8 as well.
• Do you see men and women being asked to take on roles in the body of Christ on the basis of the teaching Paul gives here? Or are different methods of allocation being used?

Elbows are invaluable—it's difficult to feed yourself with even a biscuit if your arms won't bend—but groups of elbows (or fingers or ears, or any single body part) don't make a very versatile team. In the same way, within the group or wider Church we'd be seriously disadvantaged without those whose personalities and gifts differ from ours.

Further study

In the world generally, but also in the Church, men and women may struggle with questions such as:

• Who am I?
• Do I belong?
• Am I of value?
• What am I here for?

There are many ways of answering these big questions, but how might you do so from the 1 Corinthians passage? Work in twos or threes, and then report back to the group.

Prayer focus

If one part suffers, every part suffers with it; if one part is honoured, every part rejoices with it.
1 CORINTHIANS 12:26

Sharing in suffering and rejoicing is possible only if there's communication between the parts of the body. Depending on the character of your group and the degree of trust and openness that already exists, either divide into threes or stay as one group. Ask each member who would like to do so briefly to share a need for prayer and/or a cause for thanksgiving to God. After each person has done so, one or more members pray for them or offer thanksgiving, and all pray silently.

Group decision
Is there anything you would like to do differently within the group in future as a result of what you've read, thought or prayed in this session?

Make sure that group members have a note of the 'homework' to be done before the next session.

Session 2

To prepare
All read 1 Peter 2:4–17 beforehand. Notice how many words in this passage emphasize the corporate nature of the people of God. (The word 'corporate' comes from *corpus*, the Latin word for body.) Can you think of other words used elsewhere in the New Testament that do the same?

Together as one

Learning activity

Joined together as one in the body of Christ, we cannot live our lives in isolation. The idea of all moving in the same direction on parallel tracks isn't biblical.

> *'Good morning' she* says*
> *with expressionless face*
> *as we pass in the street.*
> *No sense of belonging—*
> *just parallel people*
> *who never will meet.*
>
> (* ALTERNATIVELY, HE)

Provide each group member with a copy of this short poem, which I wrote some years ago. Sit quietly and consider what feelings are evoked by the idea of 'parallel people' who never touch one another's lives. Are there any echoes in your own experience?

Divide into pairs, and share as much as you are willing. Try to share feelings, not just ideas. Decide who will share first, and then listen to each other carefully *without interrupting.* Set a time limit—for example, five minutes each. Afterwards, ask if people found it easy to listen without interrupting.

Study time

Ask someone to read John 17 out loud. It's the prayer Jesus prayed on the night before his death. He prayed for his disciples, and then for all future disciples, that they might be one. Split into threes or fours to study it in detail.

- How many times does Jesus mention 'unity' or 'being one' in this prayer?
- What reasons does he give for his request?

- What standard of unity does Jesus set?
- What help is available to those whom Jesus prays will know this unity?

Bring the small groups back together, and share your answers.

Further study

The Lord's Supper is a vivid reminder to us of our oneness in Christ. Each of the synoptic Gospels records its institution by Christ himself (Matthew 26:26–28; Mark 14:22–24; Luke 22:19–20). In his first letter to the Corinthians, Paul passes on what he received from the Lord about it (11:23–26).

Read 1 Corinthians 10:16–17 out loud. You may find THE MESSAGE version helpful as well:

When we drink the cup of blessing, aren't we taking into ourselves the blood, the very life, of Christ? And isn't it the same with the loaf of bread we break and eat? Don't we take into ourselves the body, the very life, of Christ? Because there is one loaf, our many-ness becomes one-ness—Christ doesn't become fragmented in us. Rather, we become unified in him. We don't reduce Christ to what we are; he raises us to what he is.

1 CORINTHIANS 10:16–17

Against this background, consider this question (source unknown):

'When the body of Christ is divided, who bleeds?'

Prayer focus

Discuss how you would like to pray as a group in response to the poem, the passages of scripture, the questions and answers. Then move into a time of open prayer, or write out a prayer or prayers to be said together.

Session 3

To prepare

Read John 13:34—15:17. Also, take time to observe when waiting in a queue or sitting in a crowd. Look at the body language of those around you. What do you notice? Don't assume that you know exactly what everyone is feeling from their body language. It's a clue, but not the whole picture.

Bankrupt without love

Opening prayer

When we see the standard Jesus sets for our *agape*-love, it's easy to feel a failure. It's an area in which the Evil One delights to find opportunity for discouragement—so, before you begin, pray for God's protection. Ask the Holy Spirit to lead you into truth and to fill each one with the love of Jesus as you study and share together.

Group activity and study time

Ask someone to read 1 John 4:7–21. Go through the passage again, slowly. Take it in turns to note the phrases or part-sentences including the word 'love' (or a variation of the word). Ask someone to list them on a large piece of paper, using a thick felt-tip pen so that everyone can see.

• What can be learned from this list?

Earlier, John had written, 'How great is the love the Father has lavished on us, that we should be called children of God! And that is what we are!' (1 John 3:1). Repeat this verse out loud together, and aim to commit it to memory. Accepting and remembering the love God has for us will help us to love others.

Further study

Read out Eugene Peterson's summarizing sentence which comes at the end of 1 Corinthians 13:1–3 in THE MESSAGE: 'No matter what I say, what I believe, and what I do, I'm bankrupt without love.'

Now look up these verses in the other version(s) you use. See them in the context of the whole of 1 Corinthians 13, but keep the phrase 'bankrupt without love' as your main focus. Share your responses to this phrase in threes or fours, or in the main group.

Prayer focus

So soon after being full of confidence (John 13:37), Peter had denied his Lord three times and then seen him crucified. He'd found the tomb empty, but then Jesus had appeared behind closed doors—twice. 'Oh, for a bit of normality!' thinks Peter. 'Let's go fishing!' In an event that must have reminded Peter of his original call to follow Christ (Luke 5:1–11), Jesus reached out to him across the depths of his failures and gave him a trusted role to play.

Read John 21:1–19 out loud in the group, while everyone sits quietly with eyes closed. Ask them to visualize the scene, and to hear Jesus speaking to Peter. Pray a short prayer inviting the Lord Jesus to come and speak to each one, and remain quiet with eyes closed while he does so.

Close by praying for one another silently in the main group. Ask each to pray first for the person on their left, and then for the person on their right, that they will be able to receive and share more of God's love in the coming week.

Session 4

To prepare

Read John 12:1—13:17. In addition, listen to people around you talking about what they do. Don't just listen to the words—try to hear the feelings as well. For example, what lies behind 'I'm only a housewife', or 'I'm too old to be of much use these days'?

Serving the Servant King

Learning activity

Ask group members to role-play the difference between serving a meal and dumping it down on the table in front of someone. If we're told that the person to whom we're serving the meal is Jesus, will that make a difference?

Study time

Set the scene (as covered in the 'homework' reading): Jesus had been anointed 'for burial' by Mary at Bethany (John 12:1–8); the next day he'd made a triumphal entry to Jerusalem (12:12–15); his following had grown rapidly, to the consternation of influential people (12:19); a voice from heaven had spoken in response to Jesus' prayer to his Father (12:27–29); many had confessed their faith, but some feared what might happen if they did (12:42–43). Given the circumstances, I think I might have been looking forward to a traditional celebration of the Passover among friends, a pleasant gathering with no surprises. But then…!

Each read John 13:1–17 silently. Remain silent for about ten minutes. Try to visualize the scene. Imagine the thoughts and feelings of those assembled—and the way these changed as Jesus moved among them.

Ask someone to read John 13:1–17 out loud.

Jesus made it clear that one of the reasons he washed his disciples feet was to demonstrate the upside-down values of the Kingdom of God (see also Luke 22:24–27). Then he said, 'Do as I have done for you' (John 13:15).

* How might these values be demonstrated today? Some folk seem to think that only those who work in churches or Christian organizations can (a) reveal Christ, and (b) demonstrate Kingdom values, to those around them. What about those who serve as garage mechanics, homemakers, teachers, taxi drivers, cleaners,

care assistants, social workers, accountants, refuse collectors, police officers… and in the jobs (paid or unpaid) done by group members?

Heart-attitudes matter—and not just at work. What about in family situations? As shown by the learning activity, the spirit in which ordinary things are done is important.

• Are you willing for the Lord to challenge you about what's in your heart as you serve him in all you do?

Further study

Continuing to think about serving jobs and roles, read out the list of 'good deeds' in 1 Timothy 5:10.

• Are you aware of any tendency to discount home-based serving?

Many would see only those in menial jobs as having a 'servant' role. Is this a biblical view? Jesus, the King of kings with a servant heart, surely extends our ideas about servanthood in all directions.

• Is there a need to repent of having to some extent absorbed the world's attitudes to serving?

Prayer focus

Pray for those who serve you in diverse ways.

• Pray for your church leaders.
• Pray for those you know whose jobs might bring pressures to abandon servant attitudes and to assume the world's values.
• Pray for those who struggle to see themselves as worthy of any role at all. You may like to use Ephesians 2:10 to affirm their worth as a Creator-made masterpiece, made for a purpose.
• Pray for one another, asking for help to hear what the Lord is saying about servant attitudes, and to know how to respond.

Session 5

To prepare

Read Acts 27:1—28:16. Think of times when you've been encouraged by hearing others' stories of God's faithfulness.

Encouraging one another

Learning activity

Think back to Session 3 and the verse committed to memory (1 John 3:1). Say it out loud together, with Bibles open if necessary.

Study time

Briefly outline the context of Luke 24:13–35. Then ask three group members to read the passage, one acting as narrator, one taking the voice of Jesus, and one the voices of his followers.

Encourage group members to pick out some key points. They might note, for example, that Jesus met with two of his followers who were at a low ebb, and walked with them on their journey. He would have known their circumstances, yet he allowed them to tell their story, to share their disappointment in their own words. 'We had hoped...', they said (v. 21). They'd heard the truth (vv. 25–26) but had been unable to receive it. Trudging alongside and using the scriptures, Jesus helped them to make sense of what had been going on. On reaching their village, he made as if to continue his journey. They pressed him to stay, so he did—until he'd become known to them through his breaking of the bread. Fired up by this encounter with their risen Lord, they rushed the seven miles back to Jerusalem.

• What can we learn from this picture of accompanying?

'Using the scriptures' needs to be done sensitively, speaking God's word into situations according to his leading—not using selected verses merely to add weight to our own views. Can group members give examples from their own experience of how they've been helped by a friend bringing encouragement or edification from the scriptures? If not, would they like to be helped in this way?

Further study

Ask someone to read Exodus 18:5–27 to the group.

Encouragement comes in many forms. Moses was helped by his father-in-law's observation that he was finding his job difficult because he was attempting the impossible on a daily basis. Moses needed to share the load.

- What can be learned from this story?
- Are you aware of brothers and sisters in Christ who have become discouraged—maybe even come to see themselves as failures—because they've been carrying an impossible load?

Prayer focus: Writing a prayer-psalm

Provide group members with pens and paper. Invite everyone to write their own prayer-psalm, as a way of communicating with—speaking to and hearing from—God. It can be any length, and doesn't have to be finished during the meeting.

In his introduction to the Psalms in THE MESSAGE, Eugene Peterson assures us that, whatever our polished translations may lead us to imagine, the original language of the psalms was earthy and rough. Allow your heart to speak as you write. It will be between you and God; you won't have to show it to anyone else.

Where would you like to start? You could begin with 'I had hoped…', expressing to God the hopes you have had. Maybe something is on your mind, and you'd rather start there. Perhaps you want to praise God or to thank him for something. Don't forget to hear what the Lord has to say to you as you write, and include that, too.

As you approach the end of your meeting, come back together again and pray for one another. You could use the encouraging verses from the end of Jude's letter (vv. 24–25) as a closing prayer.

Session 6

To prepare

The final chapter of most of Paul's letters (Romans to Philemon) includes personal greetings. Read some of them, and try to imagine the feelings of the original recipients as they heard their names read out.

Keep your eyes and ears open for anyone who might be in need of encouragement. In your prayer times, lift them before the Lord, and ask him if there is some other way you might be of service to them.

Building and being built up

Learning activity

Ask everyone to imagine (alternatively, ask three members to role-play) the following situation:

You've invited your group to a meal. You go into the butcher's shop, where the carcasses are stamped with the name of the pagan temple at which they've been offered in sacrifice. Over to one side, there's a heap of unmarked joints, but you know they've probably come from a similar source. A friend who has come with you reckons it would be better to choose from this unmarked selection. Through the shop window you can see another friend who has refused to come in. He or she is praying fervently that you won't buy anything at all!

• What would *you* do?

Study time

We're told to do all we can to build one another up. We also have to do our best not to undermine the work that God is doing in the lives of our fellow Christians.

Read 1 Corinthians 8:1–13 and 10:23—11:1 out loud in the group.

- From the passages, draw up a list of general principles which could be applied in the situation you imagined or role-played earlier.
- Pick out a few key verses which you feel sum up the priorities.
- Any surprises?
- Are group members facing similar dilemmas today in their work or family situations?

Further study

Ask someone to read 2 Timothy 1:1–14 out loud in the group.

- Identify the ways in which Paul builds Timothy up and encourages him in these few verses. (You may find it helpful to refer to Chapter 6 for examples of what 'building up' may include.)
- How does Paul remind Timothy of his own responsibility for being built up?

Group decision

Are there aspects of the way you relate or work together as a group which you'd like to review in the light of what you've been thinking about?

Prayer focus

Pray for one another, after sharing concerns and prayer needs. You may like to close by reading out Hebrews 13:20–21, saying 'us' in place of 'you', as your prayer for one another.

Session 7

To prepare

All read 2 Timothy. How many times does Paul express the hope that he'll see Timothy again soon?

Is there someone you haven't seen for a while to whom you could send an encouraging card or letter?

Running the race, fighting the fight

Learning activity

If you've ever run a marathon, you'll know how welcome the drinks are! Elite athletes often have their own special concoction of minerals and nutrients waiting for them—it's one of the things their support team does to ensure an optimum performance. What about our Christian race? Are we aware of having a support team? Where are our feeding stations?

Take a large piece of paper. Down one side list the ways in which members have taken on 'nourishment' for their race in the past week (for example, reading the Bible or a Christian book; praying with a friend). Then try to tease out the different types of sustenance received (for example, feeling heartened; recognizing the need to act on something read; greater awareness of God's presence). Be aware that members may be at different stages and so finding different things helpful. Encourage everyone to share as openly as they feel able, and to listen attentively to the contributions of others. Be alert for those who feel they have nothing to contribute; avoid turning the spotlight on them, but see if you can gently draw them out.

Note: One of the strategies of the Enemy is to convince Christians that church gatherings *are the race*, when they're meant to be more like feeding stations along the way.

Study time

Read 2 Timothy 3:10—4:8.

When Paul writes that he has 'fought the good fight' (4:7)—and urges Timothy to do the same (1 Timothy 6:12)—the Greek verb is *agonizo*, to fight. It's from the same root as the noun translated else-where as 'race', 'struggle' or 'conflict', and is associated with the ancient Olympic-type contests.

Paul's letters to Timothy are God-given 'nourishment' for the race/fight, sent to a younger church leader in a difficult situation. Paul had mentored Timothy, building him up in numerous ways, preparing him for his God-given ministry which was expected to continue long after Paul's own death.

- Looking back to the list you made at the beginning, consider whether there are forms of help received by Timothy which could be added. (Note: we don't gain only from pleasant experiences.)
- Are you in a position to contribute to the spiritual nourishment of others—by your life, not just your words?

Further study

Some of what Paul wrote to Timothy was practical instruction—how to go about things—but much of it focused on *attitudes*. These are more easily caught than taught; for Timothy to pass them on, they had to be evident in him (see, for example, 2 Timothy 2:22–26).

Divide into two groups if your main group has eight or more people. Ask each group to read 1 Timothy 6. Then, concentrating on this passage but adding suggestions from elsewhere if they come to mind, list—with references—the attitudes Paul urges Timothy to encourage in others. The list will cover relationships with God, fellow Christians and those outside the Church, and attitudes to eternity as well as to the priorities of this present life.

Come back together to share what you've discovered. Then consider:

- Would you welcome more help with growing godly attitudes?

Group decision

Thinking longer-term rather than just about the past week, is there a need for a more deliberate approach to support or nourishment? How might your group as a whole and the members individually play a part in sustaining one another?

Prayer focus

Pray for one another and for the group as you aim to press on together in Christ. (You could turn words from Philippians 3:12–14 into a prayer.) If you have identified needs which are not being met, pray for wisdom to know how to respond.

Session 8

To prepare

Read Exodus 20:1–17. Reflect on how God's commands work together for the good of the community—and the good of individuals too.

God's good provisions for community

Group activity and study time

Our God who is Father, Son and Holy Spirit, the Three-in-One, is *for* community.

Read out the statements below about three types of provision from God which are good for our communities. Make sure that everyone grasps the difference between 'fruit' and 'gifts'.

• God's commandments, if obeyed, contribute to the health and well-being of our communities. (See Exodus 20:1–17.)
• The fruit of the Spirit is the character of Christ being formed in each of us, and makes true community possible. (Note: the fruit of the Spirit is singular—it's not a selection of fruits from which we may pick one or two and leave the rest. See Galatians 5:22–23.)
• Spiritual gifts equip us for serving in the body of Christ community and the wider world. (Note: our gifts differ; no one has all the gifts. See Romans 12:6–8; 1 Corinthians 12:7–11, 27–31; Ephesians 4:11–13; 1 Peter 4:9–11.)

Explore these statements in one of two ways:

1) Divide into three groups, giving each a note of one of the statements and the verses following it. If your total group has less than six members, leave out the first statement, which was covered by the homework.

Ask the members of each small group to work together, using their diverse gifts, skills, personalities and life experience, to plan how they will explain or illustrate their statement, or an aspect of it, to the rest of the main group. Each presentation should take *no more than five minutes*.

Allow about forty minutes for preparation. Work on improvised drama, pictures, spoken words, a combination... be creative in your communication! (Have paper and other suitable materials to hand.) All members should be able to contribute to the preparation, but not everyone need take part in the presentation. Take care to ensure that everyone understands that it's an exercise in mutual encouragement —not a performance or a competition. Given the time-scale, there will inevitably be some rough edges! Ideally, the groups should prepare in different rooms. If space is limited, would it be possible for groups to meet separately elsewhere before coming together for the presentations?

2) Some groups may not be ready to launch out on the sort of exercise described above. You could go through the statements and the scriptures together in a more conventional manner. But don't make assumptions. You could pray for the group to be willing to be more adventurous, and for the Lord to help you as you take the risk together.

Group decision
After the five-minute presentations, review what has been learned, both as a result of what has been presented and in the process of preparing together. If your group is a continuing one, discuss whether there is anything you would like to do differently within the group as a result of what has been learned in this session and more generally.

Prayer focus

Thank God for the commandments. Pray that the fruit and gifts of the Spirit will be increasingly evident in your midst.

Pray for one another. You may like to use 1 Thessalonians 5:23–24, saying 'us' and 'our' instead of 'you' and 'your', as part of your prayer time.

Also by Pamela Evans

Driven Beyond the Call of God
Discovering the rhythms of grace

'In attempting to serve the church and our neighbour with all our hearts, minds and strength, we can find ourselves sucked into a lifestyle which undermines our very purpose and makes nonsense of our message.'

This powerful book shows how, rather than presenting the Good News, 'church' can sometimes be very bad news indeed. Christians may find themselves driven towards burn-out, becoming so absorbed in the process of worshipping and serving God that they lose sight of him altogether.

Drawing on years of pastoral experience, the author explores a right view of God and shows how his true requirements of us actually produce good mental and spiritual health. She shows, too, how we need an experience of his grace—a gift we cannot earn, however hard we try. And a helpful study section encourages us to reflect on the pace, direction and motivation of our lives, and work with others towards a healthier style of discipleship.

ORDER FORM

REF	TITLE	PRICE	QTY	TOTAL
0545	*Driven Beyond the Call of God*	£7.99		

POSTAGE AND PACKING CHARGES					
order value	UK	Europe	Surface	Air Mail	
£7.00 & under	£1.25	£3.00	£3.50	£5.50	
£7.01–£30.00	£2.25	£5.50	£7.50	£11.50	
Over £30.00	free	prices on request			

Postage and packing:

Donation:

Total enclosed:

Name _____ Account Number _____

Address _____

_____ Postcode _____

Telephone Number _____ Email _____

Payment by: Cheque ☐ Mastercard ☐ Visa ☐ Postal Order ☐ Switch ☐

Credit card no. ☐☐☐☐ ☐☐☐☐ ☐☐☐☐ ☐☐☐☐ Expires ☐☐ ☐☐

Switch card no. ☐☐☐☐☐☐☐☐☐☐☐☐☐☐☐☐☐☐

Issue no. of Switch card ☐☐☐☐ Expires ☐☐ ☐☐

Signature _____ Date _____

All orders must be accompanied by the appropriate payment.

Please send your completed order form to:
BRF, First Floor, Elsfield Hall, 15–17 Elsfield Way, Oxford OX2 8FG
Tel. 01865 319700 / Fax. 01865 319701 Email: enquiries@brf.org.uk

Available from your local Christian bookshop. BRF is a Registered Charity

www.brf.org.uk

Enter an author, title, subject or phrase

Books ○
Extracts/Info ●

go

brf
Resourcing your spiritual journey

Home
Bible Centre
Book news
Events
Articles
Authors
Who is BRF?

Welcome to BRF

For Bible based resources and information for today's Christian living and for details of all BRF publications, extracts and articles, and a wealth of other information.

Find out about:
- New BRF publications
- BRF's comprehensive range of resources:
  Bible reading and study; Prayer and spirituality; Lent and Advent
- BRF authors
- Quiet days, Retreats and other events
- Barnabas (storybooks, seasonal activity books and teaching resources for 3–11 year olds)
- The Barnabas Live Creative Arts and Schools Programme

The Bible Reading Fellowship
First Floor
Elsfield Hall
15–17 Elsfield Way
Oxford
OX2 8FG
England
Tel 01865 319700
Fax 01865 319701
E-mail
enquiries@brf.org.uk

Visit the BRF website at www.brf.org.uk